Timin
Financial
Charting your way to profit

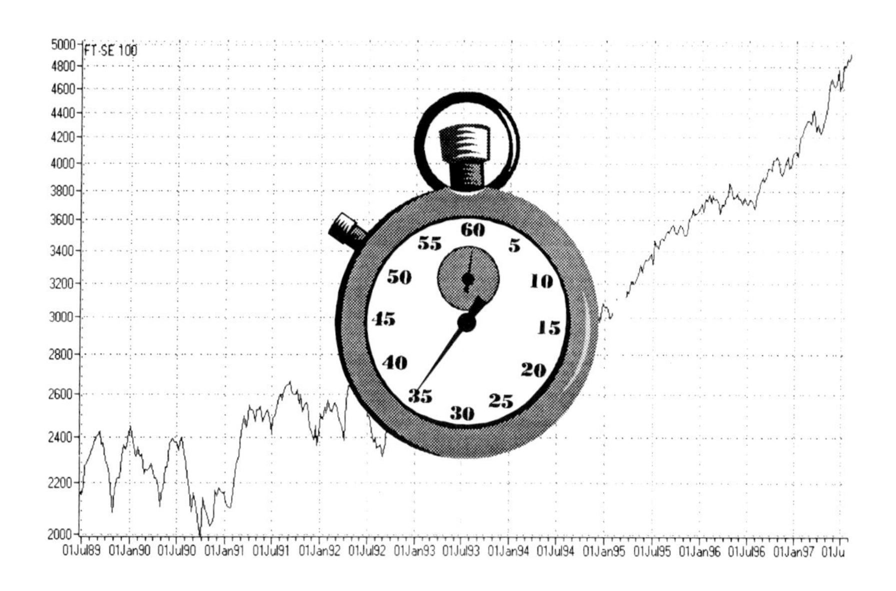

Alex Kiam

TAKE THAT LTD.

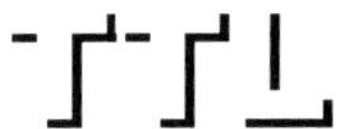

Take That Ltd.
P.O.Box 200
Harrogate
HG1 2YR
sales@takethat.co.uk
www.takethat.co.uk
Fax: +44-1423-526035

10 9 8 7 6 5 4 3 2 1

You should take independent financial advice before acting on material contained in this book.

Printed and bound in Great Britain.

ISBN 1-873668-47-3

Contents

Author's Preface

The difference between the investor and a trader is all down to time and timing. An investor puts his money into the financial market and leaves it there with a view to riding out the highs and the lows. This is, of course, a sensible strategy and one that history shows will produce better returns than leaving your money on deposit. The trader, on the other hand, looks at the fluctuations and volatility of the financial markets and aims to make full use of them. The rising market is a chance to make money by buying at low prices and selling at high. And a falling market is also a chance to make money by selling at high prices and buying again at low.

I have never met a successful short-term trader who is not also a very successful long-term investor. But I have met many investors who simply can't hack it as traders. The reason is simple. Investing makes money almost by default providing you don't panic and lose your head when all around you are losing theirs. But trading is about making sure you don't get caught out by crashes while making the most of your opportunities along the way. To achieve this you need a firm understanding of technical analysis, which you will gain from reading this publication, along with a different set of personal characteristics which are discussed in more detail in Chapter 12.

Technical analysis is accepted as a valid and useful approach to the financial markets by virtually all commentators. Indeed, the widespread use of trading programmes by brokerage firms is testament to its power. These days large investments are simply not made without reviewing the technical chart.

Even if you are slightly sceptical about some of the analysis techniques you have to accept that it is a self-fulfilling prophecy. Simply because so many brokerage firms use technical analysis the prices will react in a way that will conform to technical analysis. When a chart shows that a certain financial instrument should be sold the brokers go ahead and sell. This process, of course, depresses the price of that financial instrument showing that they were right to bail out in the first place.

Very few individual traders have the same resources available to them as the top brokerage firms. That means that they can't possibly hope to keep up with them across the whole range of the financial market. But this in itself offers an opportunity. Instead of being a jack-of-all-trades you can specialise in certain stocks or other financial instruments and concentrate on one or two indicators from those available. In this manner you will become an "expert" in a particular corner of the market and find that you can react quicker and more consistently than even the largest of investment houses. And it is not difficult. The approach you need to take can be summarised in four simple steps:

- ✔ Use charts to determine the overall trend of the market.
- ✔ Pick a few financial instruments which show reasonably large fluctuations in price and with which you are familiar,
- ✔ Use your charts to determine the trends and cycles of your chosen financial instruments, and
- ✔ Pick your buying and selling points using your favourite indicators.

Technical analysis isn't, of course, a blue-print for easy profit. It will not guarantee a profit and isn't an answer to all your investment woes. It will, however, reduce your risk and improve your overall profits. A lot of your success will come from experience and by refining your techniques over time. But even before you perfect your technique you will be gaining an advantage over your fellow investor. Because even though it is accepted by all the market professionals and learned institutes, very few individuals perform even the most basic forms of technical analysis.

By buying this book you have shown that you are different and you have certainly taken the first step towards timing the markets like a professional trader.

Chapter 1

Technical Analysis

Technical analysis is not as complicated as it may sound. Indeed, it is not very technical and does not require a great deal of analysis. It is a very basic approach to investing centred around the study of price fluctuations. Price and volume charts are the tools of the trade and are used to indicate when you should buy or sell a financial instrument. If you get it right, and time the markets correctly, you will be able to profit whether the markets are rising or falling. And, as you will find out in Chapter 10, you can even make money when they are neither rising nor falling.

Hundreds of years of charts have shown that the prices on financial markets tend to move in trends. These trends are merely indicators of an imbalance in the supply and demand of those financial instruments. If demand outstrips supply the price will rise, and if supply outstrips demand the price will fall.

The problem comes in the fact that these exchanges of financial instruments (through buying and selling) are carried out by humans, and humans are not always predictable. They do, however, follow a certain herd instinct, and if you look at large groups of humans such as all those trading on the worlds financial markets, you will see that they do remarkably similar things over long periods. This is not, perhaps, too surprising if you consider that we all have two arms, two legs, one head and one brain. We require food and drink to keep us alive, and we will all grow old and die.

Bearing this herd instinct in mind it is therefore less important that you should study the fundamentals behind a financial instrument (in an effort to understand what value it should have) than trying to discover what price other investors will put on it.

If you know that everyone else thinks £5 is too low a price for a particular share then you will buy every time the price approaches that value. You do this in the knowledge that other investors will perceive it as a bargain and enter the market as buyers and so push up the price. Similarly if you knew that all other investors consider £10 to be too high a price for that share you will sell every time it approaches £10 knowing that there will be lots of other investors about to dump their stock.

Of course, you can't pick up the phone and ask everybody else what they think about all the financial instruments that are on offer. (If you do think this is a good idea please let me know first so I can purchase some shares in the Telecom's sector). So the only indicator that you have available to you, as to what other investor's expectations are, is a chart of historical data.

Charts of price changes show you, in great detail, exactly what other investors thought at the time. If they had thought any different then the laws of supply and demand would have caused the chart to take on a different profile. As Charles Dow pointed out in 1887, a financial instrument's price reflects everything that is know about it. As new information comes into the market buyers and sellers as a whole quickly absorb the information and adjust the price accordingly. So by using charts to see what groups of humans have done in the past you will be able to make a good prediction of what they are likely to do in the future.

Don't be fooled, though, into thinking that technical analysis is a guaranteed way of predicting the movements of financial markets. It is more of an art than a science and there will always be an element of unpredictability. This is what makes the markets so exciting and means that one trader will make more money than another. Whilst the best approach is to use one or two charting techniques in combination with your in-depth knowledge of one or two stocks, you should also be aware of other patterns and indicators that are in common usage.

By taking a combined approach to the markets you will never be caught off-guard and there should be very few nasty surprises just around the corner.

The following pages will teach you the basics of technical analysis. Starting with prices and charts which are the tools of the trade and leading through trends, support and resistance, moving averages, and reversal patterns you will see how charting can improve your timing of the markets. Then, by learning how to use oscillators and indicators, as well as understanding the markets through market momentum, sentiment and monetary indicators, you will improve your overall performance. Once you have taken onboard these basic principles, the book will look at slightly more in-depth analysis techniques which concentrate on the time element of the markets and cycles in particular. It ends up with a brief discussion of chaos theory and some personal thoughts on a what makes a successful chart trader.

So what are you waiting for? Money is waiting to be made.

Chapter 2

Dow Theory

The grandfather of technical analysis is undoubtedly Charles Dow who developed two broad market averages in 1887. These were the Industrial Average which included 12 blue chip stocks, and the Rail Average which was made up of 20 railroad companies. These averages are still on the go today and are known as the *Dow Jones Industrial Average* and the *Dow Jones Transportation* Average respectively.

Charles Dow published a series of articles in the *Wall Street Journal* between 1900 and 1902 These were subsequently brought together by Dow's successor as editor of The Journal, William Hamilton, to formulate The Dow Theory. Whilst there is little evidence that Dow intended his theory to become anything more than a way of using stock market trends as an indicator for general business conditions, it ended up as the predecessor of almost all the principles of modern technical analysis.

The Dow Theory comprises six essential principles...

The Averages Discount Everything

As new information arrives into the stock market all participants quickly disseminate the information and prices are adjusted accordingly. Therefore an individual share price reflects everything that is known about that security. The same price also includes everything that is foreseeable and every condition that can affect the supply and demand in the future.

The Three Trends

At any given time there are three trends unfolding in the stock market:

- The primary trend which usually lasts for more than a year,
- The secondary trend which is a corrective reaction to the primary trend and typically last for one to three months (usually retracing up to two thirds of the previous secondary trend),
- The tertiary trend or minor trend which is a short term movement lasting from one day to three weeks. The complete Dow Theory indicates that short term price fluctuations are unimportant and can be misleading.

Primary Trends Have Three Phases

Each primary trend, according to Dow Theory, is made up of the three phases...

❶ First there is aggressive buying by well informed investors ahead of economic recovery and really long term growth. Most investors at this point have a negative attitude towards the market and are the suppliers of the stock which is being bought by the "smart money".

❷ The second phase is indicated by improving company earnings and generally better economic conditions. During this phase the majority of investors start to buy into the market.

❸ The third phase is characterised by record earnings and peak economic conditions. Having seen the market rise and rise, the general public are now tempted to participate and enter the market in a head long rush. Although prices are rising those well informed investors who were buying in the first phase are now beginning to sell in anticipation of the inevitable downturn.

Principle of Confirmation

No change in trend of either of the averages is valid unless it is confirmed by the other. So a rising trend in one average cannot be confirmed until the other average also shows a rising trend.

Volume Confirms the Trend

Rallies in the market are accompanied by increasing volume, and falls with decreasing volume. Note: The Dow Theory does not allow volume to be an indicator of the direction of the market itself, but can only act as confirmation, or otherwise, of price movement.

A Trend Continues Until a Reversal Signal

If a primary trend is confirmed by the movement of both averages it will continue until there is a definite reversal signal. So once a primary trend has started the chances are it will continue, but once it has been around for a while the chances of continuation are less.

Chapter 3

Prices and Charts

Virtually all the charts and indicators used by technical analysts are based entirely on:

a) the price of a financial instrument, and
b) the volume traded of a financial instrument.

This may sound like simplicity itself, but before you rush off and create your first charts you have to decide which "price" and which "volume" you are going to plot.

Price Fields

Open - This is the price of the first trade of the day, in other words the "opening shot". It is especially important when analysing data on a 24-hour basis since it represents a consensus price after market makers have been able to review all their data and respond to movements in other markets around the world.

High - This is the highest price at which a financial instrument is traded during the day. Higher prices may have been asked for by sellers through automated trading or on the floor, but there wouldn't have been any takers beyond the high point.

Low - This is the lowest price at which a financial instrument is traded during the day. Of course, if a lower price had been posted there will have been plenty of buyers willing to snap it up but nobody was willing to sell the instrument at such a low price.

Close - This is the final price that the instrument was traded at during the day. Since it represents the most up to date (or up to the minute) price for an instrument it is the one that is most often used in technical analysis and is quoted in newspapers as the "price of a share". The change on the day, or the difference between the opening price and closing price is of the utmost importance to the technical analyst.

Bid - This is the price that a market maker is willing to pay for a financial instrument and it is the price that you will receive if you are selling.

Ask - The opposite of the bid price. It is the price at which a market maker is willing to sell you a financial instrument and it is the price you will pay if you are buying.

Mid - This it the price midway between the bid and asking price of a financial instrument and is the price most often quoted in the financial press.

Volume Fields

Volume - This is the number of units of a financial instrument that were traded during the period. It could be the number of shares or the number of contracts. Volume is the factor most overlooked by the majority of investors but not by the professionals.

When a large volume of shares are traded you can be fairly sure that the 'price' is accurate since it represents a consensus between many buyers and sellers. But when the volume is low the price has been set by only a small number of individuals or organisations and may not be totally representative of the true 'value'.

Open Interest - This relates primarily to the futures, forwards and options markets. It is a total number of outstanding contracts that had not been closed, exercised or expired.

It is a combination of these price and volume fields that are used to create charts and indicators for the technical analyst to work on. The change between the various prices and the volume of shares or contracts traded give you an indication as to the relationship between buyers and sellers. It is easy to say that if there are more sellers than buyers then a price will go down, and vice versa. But are there a lot more sellers than buyers, or only a few more?

Your primary source of these data fields will probably be the daily newspaper. It is unlikely that all of the fields will be given for all of the instruments that you are interested in, even if you are referring to the Financial Times. A secondary source of information, and one which is useful for keeping track of prices during the day, is the Teletex and Ceefax facilities on your TV. But perhaps the most useful source for any technical analyst is the plethora of information available on the Internet. With just a little research you will be able to find all of the fields mentioned above for any instrument that you are interested in totally free of charge. Don't be put off if the first site that you find asks you to pay for the information you require, instead keep looking because I can assure you that it is all out there for free if you look hard enough (I can recommend Mark Neely's book called *Find What You Want on the Internet* on page 93, for those who are interested).

Charts

Whilst it is possible to work with the raw data, whether you get it from the newspaper or the Internet, it is far easier to make a graphical representation of the information available.

Line Charts

This is the simplest form of chart available to the technical analyst with time presented along the X-axis and price on the Y-axis. The actual time function that you plot will depend on your position in the market - a market maker will be interested in price fluctuations on a minute-by-minute basis, whilst the average investor will only be interested in a price on a daily or even weekly basis. Any price may be plotted on a line chart, but the most common is the closing, mid-price.

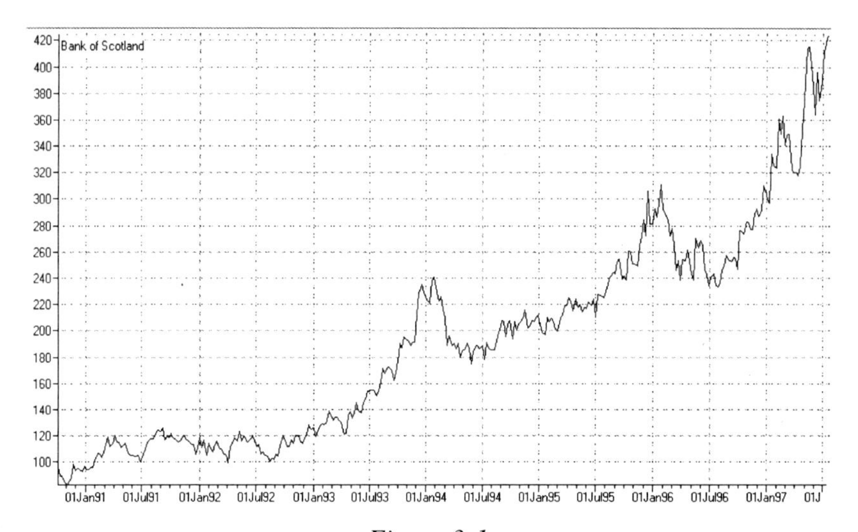

Figure 3-1
A simple line chart showing the rise in value of Bank of Scotland shares

The largest benefit to the analyst of drawing line charts are their simplicity. They present an uncluttered picture of price movements and are very easy to understand.

Bar Chart

The bar chart has similar axes to a line chart, with time along the X-axis and price along the Y-axis. But instead of a single point being put on the chart for each time period (say each day) a bar is drawn. The top of the bar is drawn at the highest price reached by the instrument during the day and the bottom of the bar is at the lowest price.

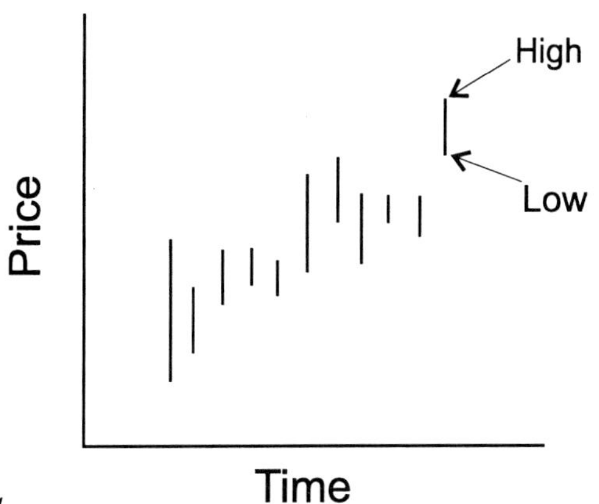

Figure 3-2a

A variation on the simple bar chart is made when opening and closing prices are available. As well as the main bar, the opening price is represented by a tick on the left side of the bar and the closing price by a tick on the right side of the bar.

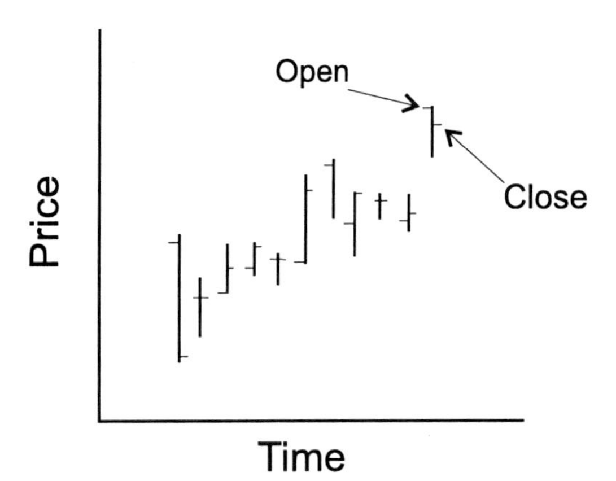

Figure 3-2b

Volume Chart

Volume is usually displayed as a bar graph along the bottom of a price chart, or on a separate chart to be viewed in conjunction with a simple price chart. Obviously time is plotted along the X-axis and volume on the Y-axis (though the volume scale is often not shown).

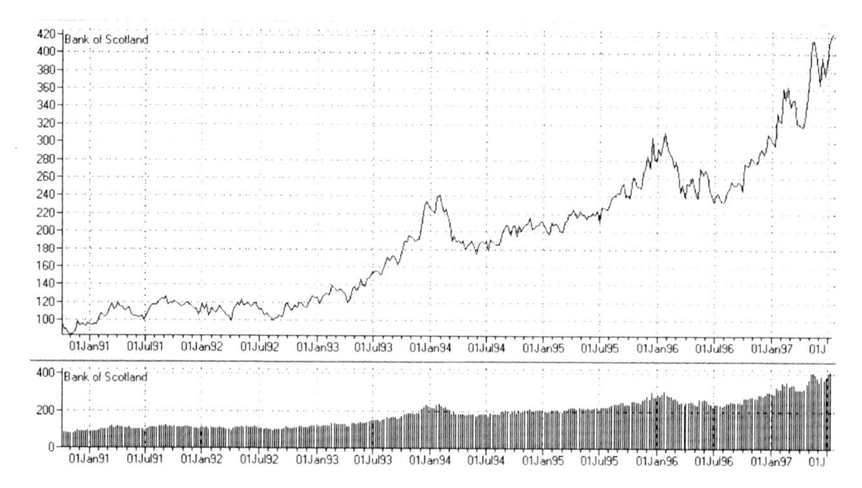

Figure 3-3 Volume associated with the movement of Bank of Scotland shares shown in Figure 3-1.

There are two accepted ways of displaying the volume of shares traded. The first is a relative level of volume which is "zero based". This means that the bottom of each volume bar is at the zero level.

The second, which most technical analysts prefer, is that of "relative adjusted" volume. This is created by subtracting the lowest volume that occurred during a trading period from all of the volume bars. So instead of the bottom of the bar representing zero it is a real figure equal to the lowest volume traded. This makes it easier to see trends in volume and monitor changes in behaviour by taking away the bulk of the "normal" volume.

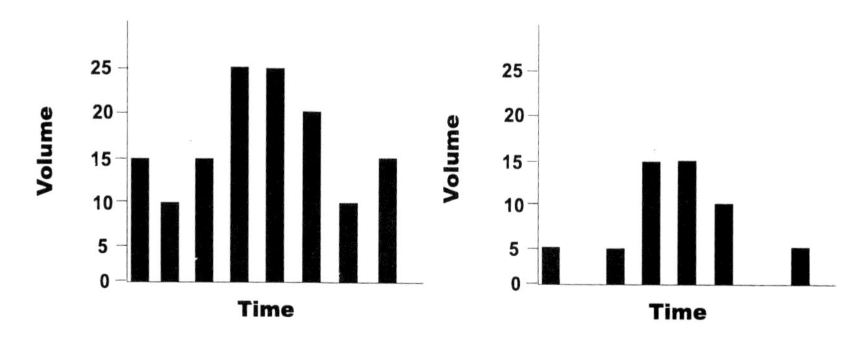

Point and Figure

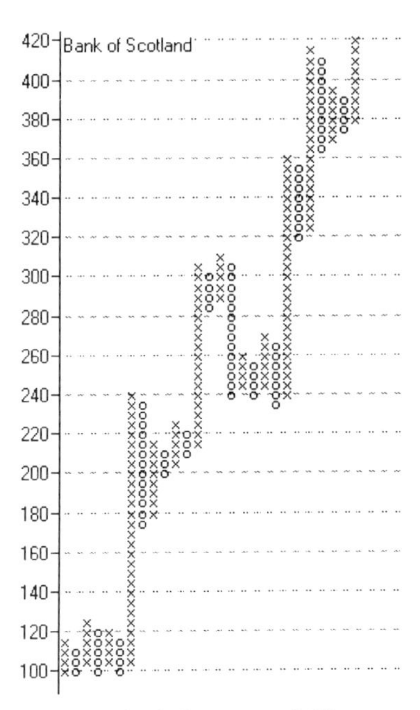

Figure 3-4 Point and Figure chart for the same Bank of Scotland price movements as shown in Figure 3-1

A Point and Figure chart, again, has price on the Y-axis and Time on the X-axis, but on this occasion the time function is not regular. Instead, every time a price rises by a certain pre-defined amount (say 5p) a cross is drawn on the chart above the previous one. If the price goes down, on the other hand, by a small amount (less than 5p) nothing is drawn. But if the price goes up again then the line of crosses will continue with one cross representing each step of 3p.

If the price falls by more than the pre-defined amount then the line of crosses stops and a new line is created, this time with noughts. Now every time the price drops by one step of 5p a nought is drawn on the chart. And, as before, a column of noughts is drawn until the price starts to increase by more than the pre-defined amount.

The idea behind this form of chart is to clarify the way in which price is "moving" by taking away the smaller or trivial price fluctuations. By choosing an appropriate step size for the value of a financial instrument, and choosing the number of steps needed to cause a reversal on the chart, only "significant" price changes will be shown.

The alternative to columns of crosses and zeros is to use chevrons pointing upwards for price increases and downwards for decreases. You will see these most often on charts printed from a computer since the resolution of many computer screens is not sufficient to distinguish between small crosses and zeros.

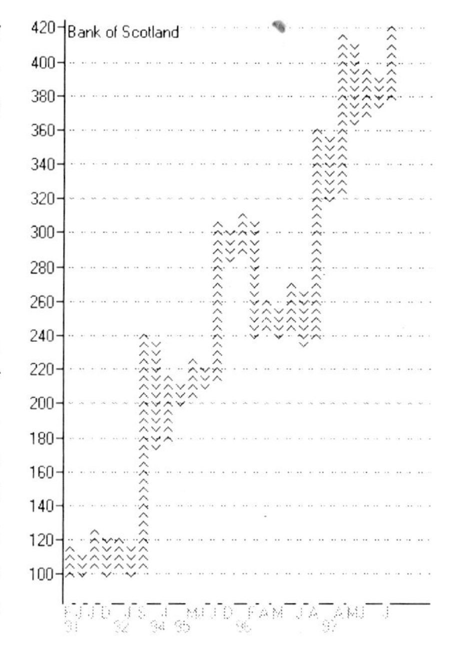

Other Forms of Chart

The four chart forms described above will encompass 95% of the charts used by most technical analysts. However there are other charting techniques used by a minority of which you should be aware, but for which the interpretation is beyond the scope of this book.

Candlesticks - This is a method of technical analysis with its roots in the trading of rice contracts in 17th Century Japan. It is similar to the bar chart in that a line is drawn from the highest price to the lowest price achieved during the day. However instead of using ticks, a horizontal line is drawn across the high-low line at the opening price, and a second line is drawn across at the closing price. The area between these two horizontal lines is now boxed and filled-in with a solid colour if the closing price is lower than the opening price. If the opposite is true, and the opening price is lower than the closing price, then the box is left empty.

High
Open
Close
Low

High
Close
Open
Low

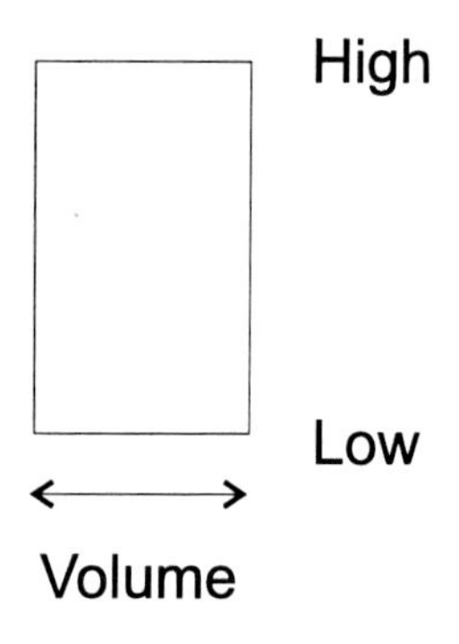

Equivolume - Displays prices in a way that suggests that volume is a driving force. Instead of simply displaying volume as a subsidiary line on a main price chart, Equivolume combines the instrument price and volume traded in a two dimensional box. The top horizontal line of the box is drawn at the highest price attained during a trading period, whilst the bottom horizontal line represents the lowest price achieved. The width of the box is determined by the volume of trades which have taken place and is a unique feature of the Equivolume charting method. It suggests that traded volume, rather than time, is the main guiding influence on the changes in price of a financial instrument.

Chapter 4

Trend Lines and Channels

Literally hundreds of years of price charts bear testament to the fact that the values put on financial instruments tend to move in trends. These trends are simply indicators of an imbalance of supply and demand of a particular instrument. When the supply of an instrument is greater than the demand there will be more sellers than buyers, and the trend will be downwards. On the other hand, when demand exceeds supply, there will be more buyers and the price trend will be upwards. Should supply and demand be roughly equal, then the market will move sideways, not producing a discernible up or downtrend, and the price of the instrument will stay within a "trading range".

There are three forms of trend:

- **Minor Trends** - Are very short lived and last for only a few days to a couple of weeks,
- **Intermediate Trends** - Lasts for a few weeks to a couple of months,
- **Major Trends** - Lasts for a period in excess of a couple of months and could be several years.

Once a trend comes to an end, then the trend that was apparent is usually reversed. So if a downtrend line is broken then it becomes a signal to buy. Similarly if an uptrend line is broken it is a signal to sell. This is made more obvious if you consider the underlying supply and demand. As discussed above the downward trend is caused by there being more sellers than buyers of a particular instrument in the market. If that trend comes to an end then you can surmise that there is no longer a surplus of sellers. Therefore the buyers are gaining an upper hand and the price will be expected to rise.

Simple Trend Lines

An uptrend line or rising trend is defined by successively higher prices for a financial instrument, with the bulls being firmly in control. There will, of course, be small oscillations in the price throughout the period of the **uptrend**. But each time the price drops slightly, due to a small correction such as profit taking, the "bottom" will be higher than the previous. So on a chart of price against time you can draw a line connecting the successive bottoms as shown in Figure 4-1.

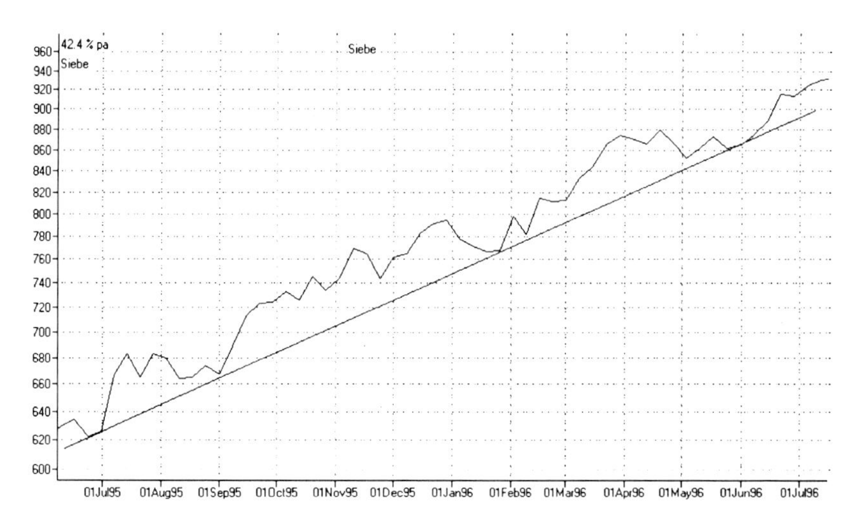

Figure 4-1 An uptrend in Siebe shares

A falling trend line or **downtrend**, is defined by successively lower prices where the buyers are in control, pushing prices lower. This time the trend line is drawn across the "tops" of the falling price. So long as the prices remain below or on this line the downtrend is in force - as show in Figure 4-2.

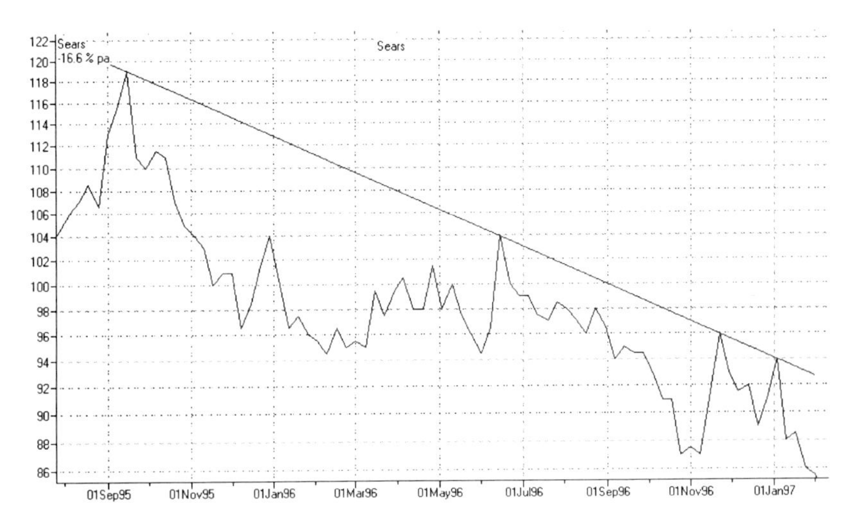

Figure 4-2 A downtrend in Sears shares

Technical analysts tend to talk about the "**authority**" or "**validity**" of the trend line. This depends on a number of factors including the number of bottoms or tops which have formed on the trend line, duration of the trend line, and the angle of the line drawn on the chart. A trend line which has a shallower angle in either direction, contains lots of bottoms or tops, and has been followed for a long time will be technically "significant" and carry a lot of authority. A very steep trend line, on the other hand, exhibiting only two or three bottoms or tops and lasting for a short period is not very authoritative and is of less technical significance. In short, the more often that prices move in such a way to test the trend line (come close to or onto the line) and the trend holds, then the more authority it will have.

The start of a trend is difficult to spot because at the beginning you will only have one top or bottom to work with. So you will have to wait for prices to move in either direction and then react again before you will get a second top or bottom. As soon as this happens you can draw a line on your chart, though you already know this will not have much authority. As time goes on another top or bottom will be formed which may confirm your trend. With just three points to work on (tops or bottoms) an exact trend will have more authority. However it is more likely that these tops or bottoms will not be exactly in line. At this point it will be possible to draw two lines on your chart. The first will be drawn from your first top or bottom to the second top or bottom, and the second from your first top or bottom to your third top or bottom. The next top or bottom that occurs will confirm which trend is in force and will give it much more authority.

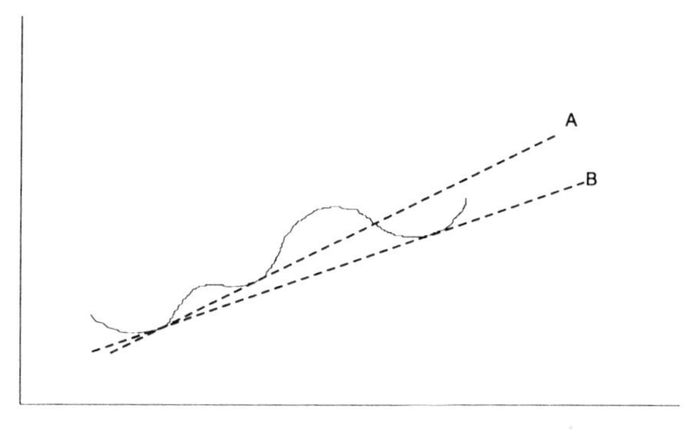

Figure 4-3a

Figure 4-3a shows this in operation in a rising market. Three tops have been generated but it is possible to draw two lines, **A** and **B**, across the tops of the data. At this point you don't know which trend is going to take hold. Progressing to Figure 4-3b you can see that another top and bottom has been created on the chart and that a trend line with more authority can now be drawn.

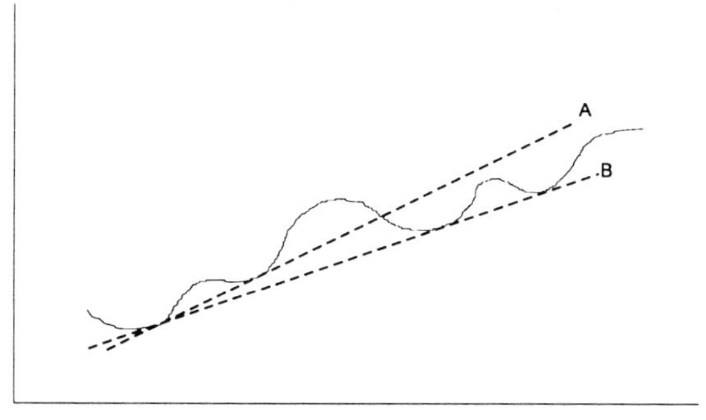

Figure 4-3b

If, when progressing from 4-3a to 4-3b the next top had not fallen as a point consistent with trends **A** or **B** then you would have had to have drawn a third line, **C**, shown in Figure 4-3c. When you get three lines on a chart like this they are known as "**fan lines**" and they indicate that a change is taking place. The general rule of thumb is that when a third fan line has been broken by the data then a trend direction will be reversed. So from Figure 4-3c you can expect a generally uptrending market to turn into a downtrend. Similarly a series of downtrends in a falling market will be reversed into an uptrend by such a break.

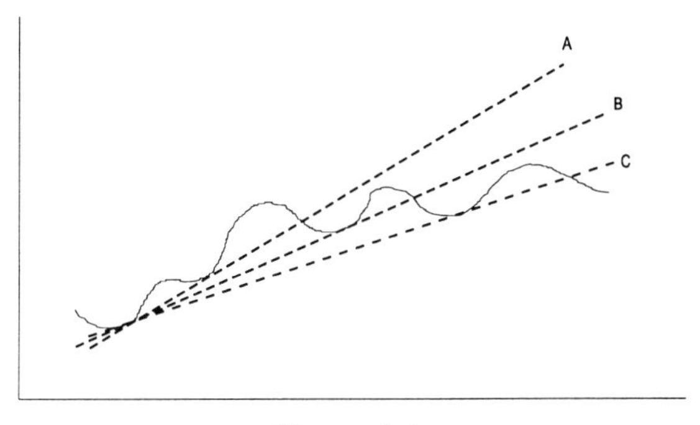

Figure 4-3c

Penetrations

Never lose sight of the fact that technical analysis is not an exact science. The instant a trend line is broken you should refrain from diving into the market and committing a lot of money. Instead you should ask yourself some questions about the validity of the penetration and then make a qualified judgement as to how convincing it is. If the penetration was only minor then it must remain questionable and you should look at other factors. For example, was the volume higher or lower on the day that penetration occurred. If volume was up then there is a good chance that the break is authentic. But if volume was down then the penetration remains questionable. You can also check to see if penetration occurred after a short period of sideways movement. If it did then this is more likely to be a testing of the trend line and the price could move in either direction. Here you would have to wait for more data before you could draw a definitive conclusion. Finally you could look for the penetration being accompanied by a reversal pattern which will be covered in Chapter 7.

Even when penetration is convincing you should refrain from committing large amounts of funds on a hunch that the opposite trend will take hold. Take this situation, for example, which is known as a **pullback**. The price of your shares have been moving on a steady uptrend for several weeks and then you notice a sharp fall in prices which decisively penetrate the uptrend. After this significant fall there is a brief rally in the value of the shares taking the price back up briefly. The bottom that has been created is off the trend line and shows that it has been broken. However before the price starts to fall again a top is created which is actually higher than the price at which the trend line was broken. If you had gone short as soon as the penetration had taken place you would be looking at a loss within a couple of days.

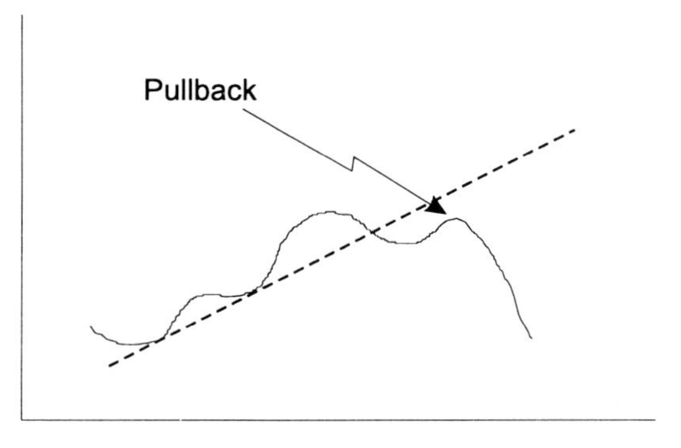

Figure 4-3d

Of course, if you wait for the pullback before you go short in order to maximise your profit then you run the risk that it will never occur and you end up selling short at a disadvantageous price. Some analysts advocate taking up half of your short position as soon as the trend line is broken and the other half when the pull back occurs. However I prefer to work to the penetration of the trend line and if I lose a little bit of extra profit by the occurrence of a pull back, then so be it. Greed has been the down fall of many an investor and I am a great believer in leaving "*a bit of profit for the next man*".

Trend Channels

When an authoritative trend is occurring it is possible to draw a second line on your chart parallel to the original trend line. This second line is drawn so that it touches the opposite feature of the price oscillation. So for an uptrend you have already drawn a line through successive bottoms. On this chart your parallel line will be drawn so that it touches a couple of tops from the same rising trend. On a downtrend the original line is drawn touching successive tops so the parallel line is made to touch the corresponding bottoms.

This second line is usually called the **return line** because it marks a point at which a price is about to return towards the trend line. The area between the original trend line and the new return line is known as the **trend channel** - see Figure 4-4a.

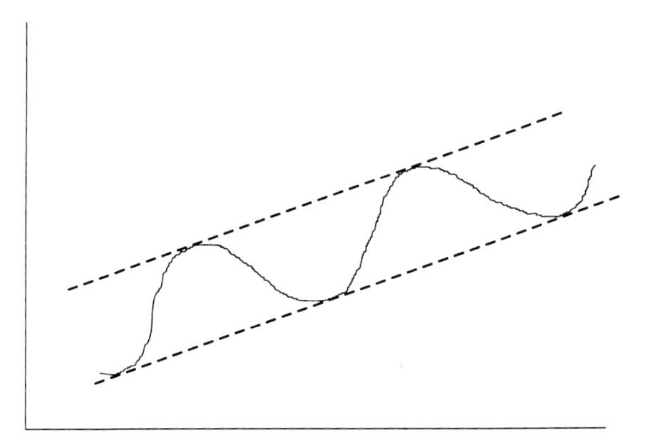

Figure 4-4a

Obviously a trend is a money making opportunity in itself. When an uptrend is in force simply buy the financial instrument in question and as long as the prices follow the trend you will be making a profit. Similarly if you sell or go short in an instrument that is on a downtrend, and then close your position out when penetration occurs, you also make a profit. However, it is possible to increase the amount of money that you make during a trend by taking advantage of the price oscillations along the way. And this is where the trend channel is most useful.

Take your chart showing your trend channel and now draw a third line parallel to and midway between your existing two lines. You have now split your channel into two "zones". The upper zone is called the **sell zone** and when the price enters this area you should sell the instrument. The lower zone is called the **buy zone** and you should buy whenever the price comes into the zone. Of course the price volatility needs to create a sufficiently wide channel for you to be able to make a profit once you have taken dealing costs into consideration.

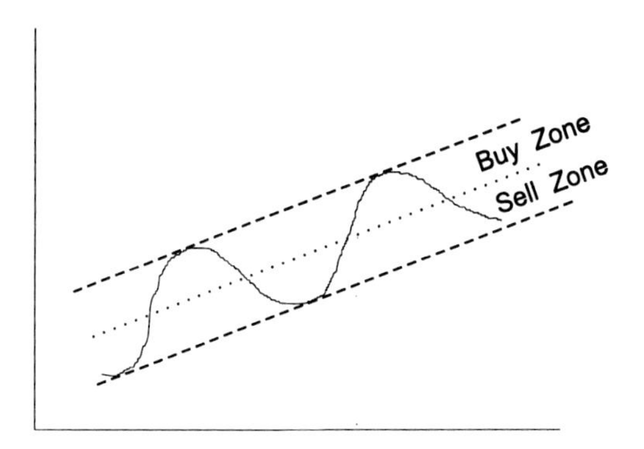

Figure 4-4b

One further use of the return line is that it can be used as a warning signal and alert you to the fact that a trend may soon be broken. If a price regularly oscillates between the basic trend and the return line, but then fails to rise as high or fall down to the return line, then you should be aware that penetration may occur next time the price approaches the original trend line.

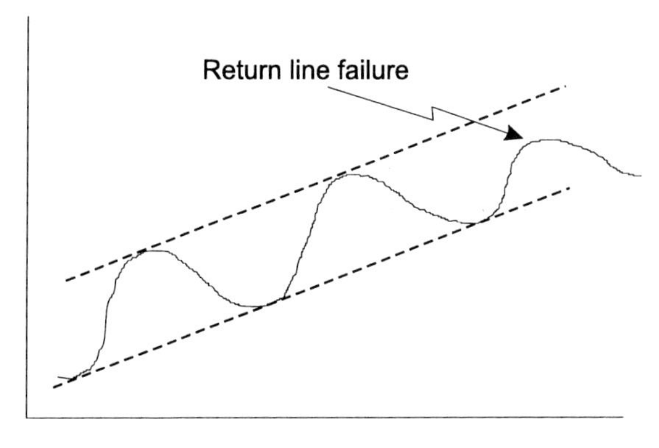

Figure 4-5

Volume

The volume, or number of shares or contracts that change hands in a given day, is an important indicator to technical analysts. This is because a large volume adds authority to any price simply because it is a consensus between a lot more people.

As you know, trends are created by an imbalance of supply and demand. When prices are rising there is more demand than supply, and when prices are falling there is more supply than demand. So to fit in with the use of volume as a gauge of the market the volume that coincides with a price increase is known as **demand volume** and the volume that occurs during a fall is known as **supply volume**.

If you think about the situation logically you will come to the conclusion that you need increasing volume for prices to go higher. If there are lots of sellers of a financial instrument, or any other product for that matter, but no buyers, then no deals can be struck and the volume will be zero. But as soon as suppliers appear and a price can be agreed, some deals will be struck, and volume will be created. As more buyers come along and volume increases there will be a relative scarcity of the stock that they want - so prices will start to increase.

Based around this principle you can create five basic rules for using volume analysis in conjunction with your trend lines:

- ✔ When prices are going up and the volume is increasing then the trend will stay in force and prices will continue to rise.
- ✔ When prices are going up and the volume is decreasing the trend is unlikely to continue and prices will either increase at a slower rate or start to fall.
- ✔ When prices are decreasing and volume is increasing then the trend will continue and prices will fall further.
- ✔ When prices are decreasing and the volume is also decreasing then the trend is unlikely to continue and the decline in prices will slow down or they will start to increase.
- ✔ When volume is consistent, not rising or falling, then the effect on prices is neutral and you need to find some other way of backing up your trend analysis.

Price	**Volume**	**Trend**
↑	↑	↑
↑	↓	→ or ↓
↓	↑	↓
↓	↓	→ or ↑
→	**n/a**	

Chapter 5

Support and Resistance

As you have seen before, the foundations of price movement are very firmly routed in the concept of supply and demand. If you remember back to your economics lessons at school, or pick up a book on basic economics, one of the first things you will notice are hundreds of graphs showing supply and demand lines.

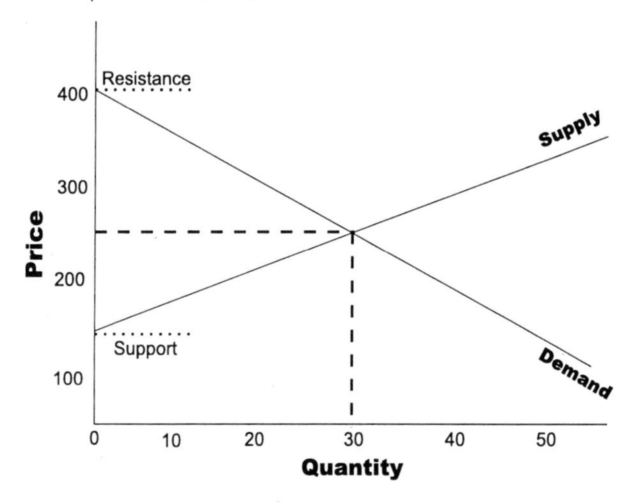

Figure 5-1 Supply and Demand

The axes generally represent the price and quantity of a product whilst the lines (or some times curves) drawn on the graph give an indication of the supply and demand for the product. For most products, which include financial instruments, the lower the price is the greater the demand will be. In other words at a price of 100p the demand will be much greater in terms of numbers than if the price was 300p.

This may seem obvious but often a graphical representation can help crystallise your thinking.

Suppliers of a product, including financial instruments, take a different approach. As a price goes up they will want to supply more of their product. Conversely, as the price falls they will be less keen to sell what they have. Most activity obviously takes place where the supply and demand lines intercept since this is where the market is in balance (around 250p in the above example).

If the market makers of the stock push the price up to around 300p you will find that demand falls off as buyers consider the price to be too high. Indeed, many investors who already have the stock will think it is a good time to sell and become suppliers. So, at this point, supply far exceeds demand and the price will fall back. If the market makers take a price in the opposite direction down to around 200p suppliers, or sellers, may consider this too low a price for their stock and will be reluctant to sell. Buyers, on the other hand, will come out of the woodwork in a bid to cash in on the bargain. In this case demand exceeds supply and the price will rise.

You can also see from the above example that there are a couple of points where sellers and buyers disappear altogether - this is where the supply and demand lines intercept with the Y-axis. At a price of only 150p there is only demand for the stock and a total absence of suppliers. This means that no bargains can be made below the price of 150p since no body is willing to sell their stock below this price. So **support** has been created for the stock at this level.

At a price of 400p, meanwhile, demand has fallen down to zero. At this price there are only suppliers who are willing to sell but nobody who is keen to buy. This time no bargains can be made above the price and a **resistance** has been created to the price moving above this point.

Of course, in a free market, the position of these lines on a graph are continually changing. As investor's knowledge and expectations about a financial instrument change, so do the prices that they are willing to buy and sell at. Higher expectations will lead to higher support and resistance levels, whilst lower expectations will see correspondingly lower support and resistance.

This head-to-head battle between buyers and sellers is one of the most noticeable and recurring events on price charts for financial instruments. Take a look at Figure 5-2.

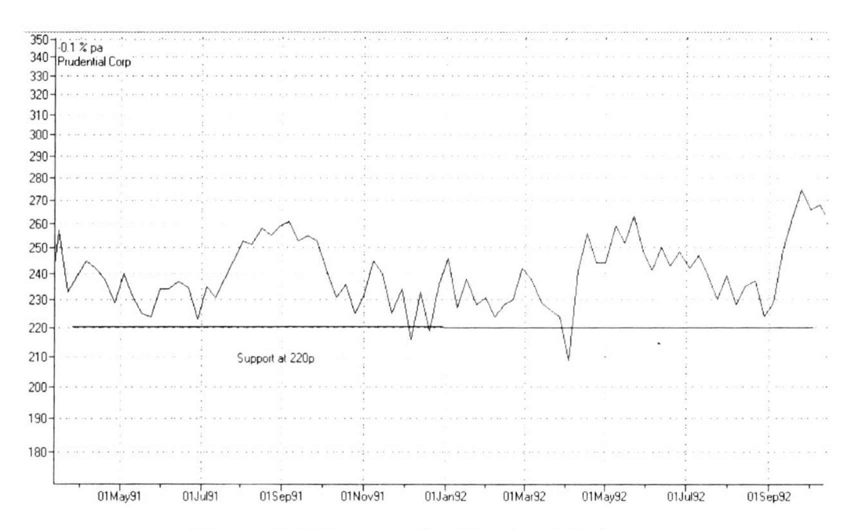

Figure 5-2 Support for Prudential shares

This shows price fluctuations in the share price for the Prudential Corporation. You can see that, over this period, every time the price approaches a level of around 220p it rebounds and increases again. In other words a support level has been set by the market at the price of 220p or thereabouts. This means that at a price of 220p the buyers feel that investing in the Prudential Corporation is a good idea and that sellers are not willing to sell their stock at a price below this level.

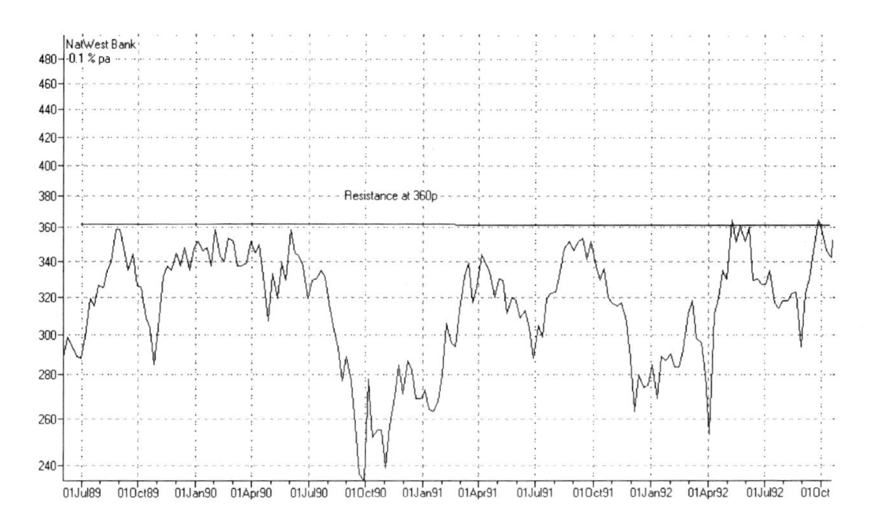

Figure 5-3
Resistance against the rise in value of NatWest bank shares

Now take a look at Figure 5-3 which shows the price movements for shares in the National Westminster Bank. You can see that a resistance level has been established at around 360p. This is the point at which sellers are taking control of the prices and preventing them from rising higher. So as soon as the price reaches a level of 360p the sellers feel that they are getting a good price for them and will dispose of their stock. At this price and above buyers are not willing to buy the shares because they do not see them as being good value.

In summary, the resistance level is a price at which the majority of investors feel the price is going to move lower and there will be at least a temporary halt in the upward movement. The support level is a price at which the majority of investors believe the price is going to move higher and there will be at least a temporary halt in the downward movement of the price.

Breakout

Casting your mind back to the discussion on supply and demand at the beginning of this chapter, you will remember that we said the lines are continually changing as investors' expectations change. So, even though support and resistance levels may be fairly firmly fixed for a particular stock, there will come a time when the market thinks that it will have enough information to warrant a change in the levels.

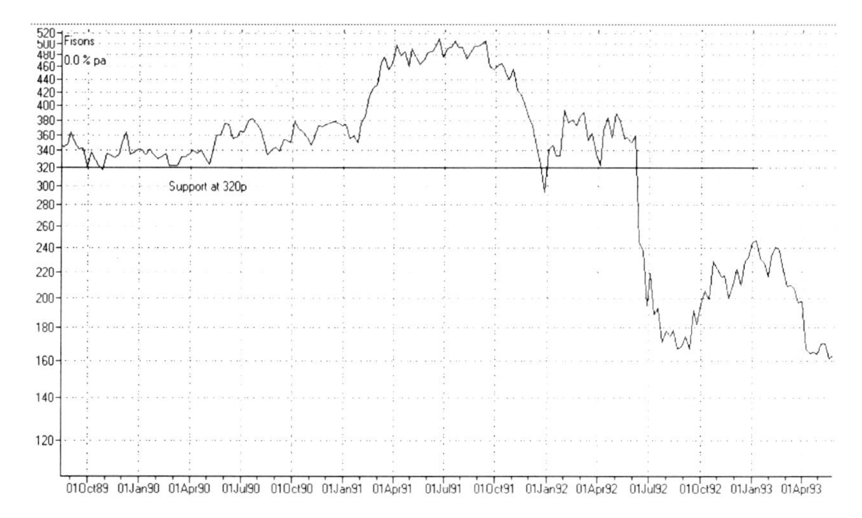

Figure 5-4 Breakout - loss of support for Fison's shares

In Figure 5-4 you will see the share price movements for Fisons during the early part of the nineties. The support level of 320p has been firmly established from late 1989 through to June 1992. Although the level was tested on several occasions the support stayed in place and the share price remained above the 320p level. Then, in June 1992, there was an abrupt change. Once investors accepted that Fison's shares could trade below the level of 320p yet more investors were willing to sell their shares and the price dropped sharply. Confidence in the stock had been damaged and buyers were no longer willing to enter the market.

The reasons for **penetration** of support and resistance levels are often rooted in a change of fundamentals underlying the value of the stock and this affects investors' expectations. But, although the trigger may be a fundamental change the sharp drop or rise in prices is a self-fulfilling prophecy.

In the Fisons example, news has entered the market which has dampened investors expectations and so the price has dropped (you can tell the news which entered the market was below investors expectations by the absolute fact that the price dropped below the support level!) This dismays owners of the shares and dampens their confidence, so they sell and the price drops even further.

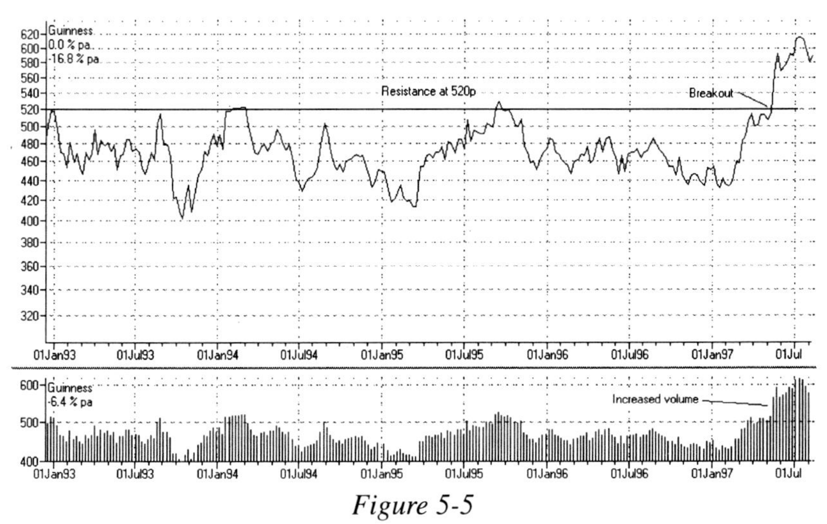

Figure 5-5
Breakout from resistance against the rise in Guinness shares

Yet again the often-ignored volume chart can help you in your assessment when a support or resistance level is being tested. Figure 5-5 shows a very well established resistance level of 520p in Guinness shares. This resistance level was in place for over four years between January 1993 and January 1997. Although it had been tested on a number of occasions the price had always dropped down and the resistance had held firm. Then in May 1997 the level was tested again, but this time there was a significant increase in volume of shares being traded. This is a prime indicator that the resistance level is about to give and the prices are about to move sharply higher. If the price had tested the resistance level but volume had stayed roughly the same, or even dropped, then you could have been fairly sure that the resistance would hold and the price would have dropped back again.

Whilst big changes are quite common once the support or resistance level is breached another effect is often visible on the price charts. This is when resistance and support swap places. In other words once the support level is broken it becomes a resistance level, and once a resistance level is broken it becomes a new support level. An example of this is shown in Figure 5-6 for Northern Foods. The support level of 260p had been established throughout the latter part of 1992 and the beginning of 1993. Then at the beginning of May bears gained the upper hand and the price broke through the support level, dropping down to 245p. It immediately bounced back again and you can see that the old support price of 260p became a new resistance level at the same price of 260p.

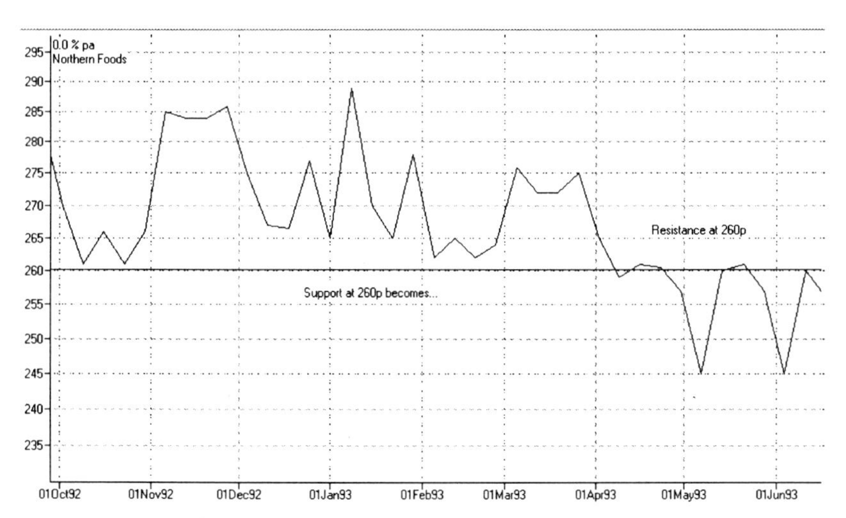

Figure 5-6 Support becomes resistance for Northern Foods

Why does this happen? The answer lies in the psychology of bulls and bears. Imagine all of the active investors in Northern Foods were grouped together. They hold the company's shares and keep an eye on the market for buying and selling opportunities. As with all investors who have a long position they are primarily hoping that the share price will rise and they will make a profit from their investment.

But in May 1993 they all caught a cold and saw the value of their investments dropping. Once the price reached 245p it started to rebound, perhaps as new buyers came into the market and realised that the stock had value. The price started to rise towards the old support level of 260p and our group of old investors seized their chance to sell their stock and so make 'less of a loss'. This action, of course, sends the price back down again, making those that didn't sell out on this occasion even more anguished. So, you guessed it, as the price inches its way up to the 260p level they, too, bail out. The price of 260p has now been firmly established as a resistance level instead of a support level.

A similar scenario takes place when a resistance level is penetrated. Those investors who have been looking for a lower price before they buy the stock realise that they have missed out as the price moves and stays higher. So each time the price falls back down towards the old resistance level they see a chance to become investors in the shares and become buyers, therefore pushing the price up again. And each time the price drops towards this new resistance level investors who missed the boat last time around will become buyers and push the price back up.

Trader's Remorse

Once a support or resistance level has been penetrated it is quite common for investors to "question" the new price levels. Here they are basically checking out the validity of the new price and seeing if it is going to stick. This phenomena is known as **trader's remorse** and sees prices returning to the old support or resistance levels not long after the price breakout. Figure 5-7 shows a price movement of ICI shares during 1994 and 1995. A support level of around 745p had been established and tested on at least three occasions, then in early 1995, breakout occurred and the price dropped below 745p. But almost immediately investors felt remorse at this treatment of the share price and values returned to their old level within a couple of weeks. This is a classical remorseful period and the market is seeing if the new lower price is warranted.

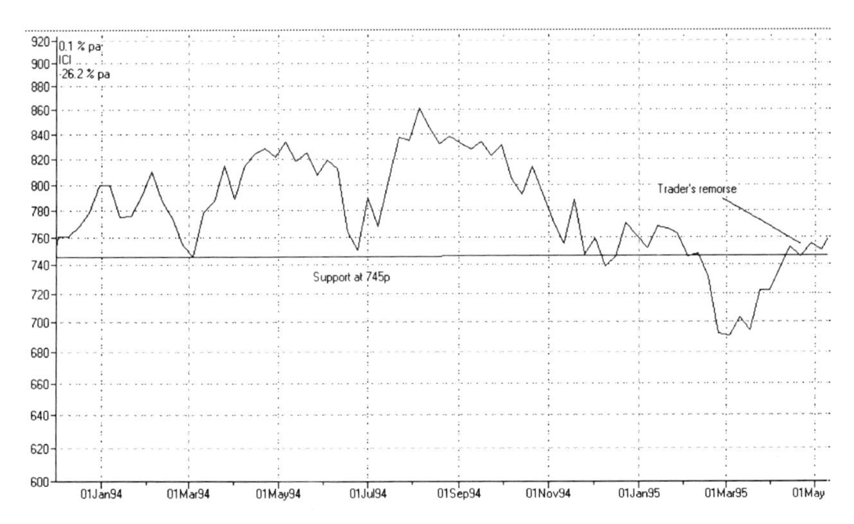

Figure 5-6 Trader's remorse over the ICI share price

One of two things can happen following a remorseful period, either:

- The market will accept that the new lower or higher price is justified, in which case prices will continue to move in the direction of the original penetration, or
- Investors will decide that the new price is not acceptable, in which case the price will move back it's earlier levels.

A false breakout, where the market's expectations decide that the new price is not actually warranted can create what is known as a **bear trap** or a **bull trap**.

You can see a classic bear trap in Figure 5-8, which is an extension of the price information given in Figure 5-7 above. You saw how the support level of 745p for ICI shares was breached in early 1995 and was followed by a remorseful period. Once the market had taken time to digest the implications of the price breaking through the old support level it obviously decided that the shares did not warrant the new lower price and they rose back to their old trading range. The price had dropped below the support level for long enough to allow bears to take a short position, expecting the breakout to herald a new era of falling prices in ICI shares. But, once the trader's remorse period was over, the price moved upwards leaving the bears staring at a loss.

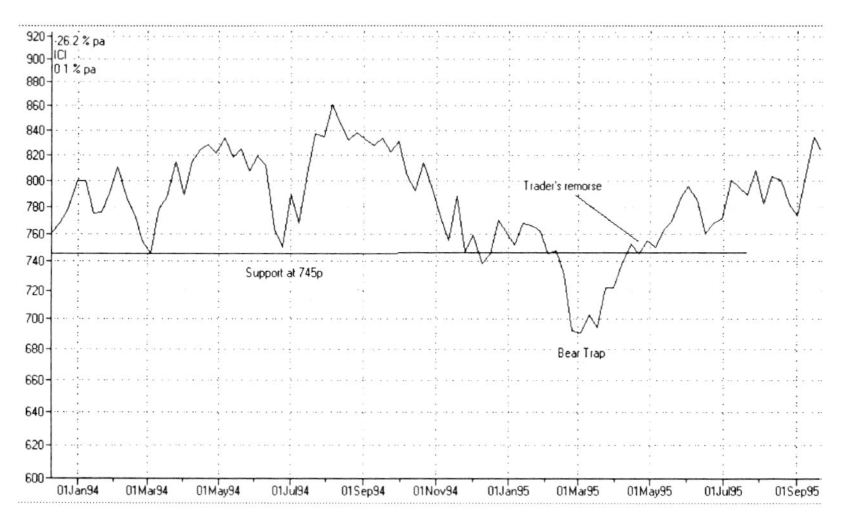

Figure 5-8 A classic Bear trap

A bull trap is caused when prices breakthrough a resistance level and then investors decide that the stock actually is not worth so much after all. The prices drop back down below the old resistance level but not before the bulls have piled into the market in the hope that the stock will continue to advance. Now, as the stock stabilises in price and the old resistance levels come back into force, it is the bulls who are left with overpriced stock and they will be forced to realise a loss.

Of course, not all remorseful periods end in a bull or bear trap. It is actually more common for the market to accept the new price it established following penetration of a support or resistance level, and firm it into an uptrend or downtrend (depending on the direction of penetration).

Figure 5-9 shows that a resistance level of 640 pence had been established for the price of Bass shares. But in July 1995 that resistance level was penetrated and shares moved up to a new level of 680p. But within a couple of weeks remorse had set in and the market moved the share price back down to 640p whilst it considered the implications of this new higher price. On this occasion it must have decided that Bass deserved a re-rating and the shares promptly set off on a firm uptrend towards the 700p level.

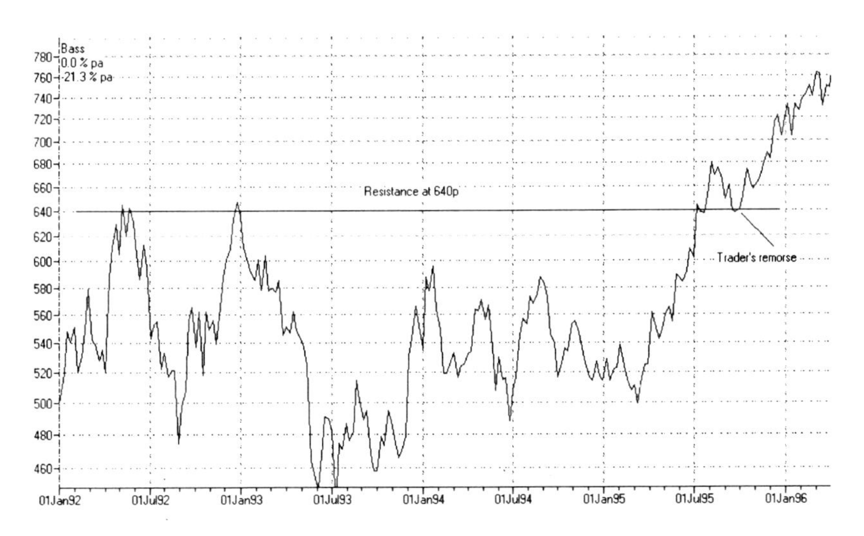

Figure 5-9 Traders accept the new trend in Bass shares

So how can you tell if a remorseful period is going to end in a "trap" or in a new trend being established? The answer, as always, lies in the accompanying volume chart. If prices break through a support or resistance level accompanied by a large increase in volume (which is usual), but the trader's remorse period shows a relatively low volume, then the new market prices are likely to become established and a trend line will set in. It shows that only a small minority of traders are remorseful about the new prices becoming established, and you can expect the majority, who show no remorse, to gain control.

On the other hand if the breakout or penetration is accompanied by a level or small increase in volume, and the remorseful period sees an increase in volume, then you can expect the prices to return to their original levels. In this scenario the majority of the market are "remorseful" about the price change and only the minority think it is valid. Again the majority will have their say and prices will return to their original levels.

Breakout volume	Remorse volume	Likely result
High	Low	New trend
Normal or low	High	Trap

Chapter 6

Moving Averages

Moving averages are one of the oldest and most popular technical analysis tools available to smaller investors. The moving average is the average price of a financial instrument at a given time. And so when you are calculating the moving average you need to specify the "time span" over which the average is calculated.

A simple moving average is calculated by adding together the closing prices of a financial instrument over a certain number of time periods and then dividing the sum by the number of periods involved. So, for example, the seven day average for a share price would be calculated by taking seven days worth of data, adding them together and dividing by seven.

Note that so far you have only calculated the seven day average of the share price and not the seven day 'moving' average. To go on and calculate the moving average you need to have, in this example, at least eight days worth of data. You start it by taking the first seven days worth of data and calculating the average value. This is now your first point on the moving average curve.

Once you have plotted this, return to your data and drop off the first or earliest data point from your original seven, leaving you with the six most recent values. Now add the latest piece of information to the six that you have been left with (in other words your eighth point) to give you a new set of seven. Take the average, again, of these new seven pieces of data (data points 2-8) to give you your second point on the moving average curve. The third moving average point will be calculated by taking the average of data from points 3-9 inclusive, the fourth will be an average of 4-10 inclusive, etc.

Calculating a Seven-day Moving Average

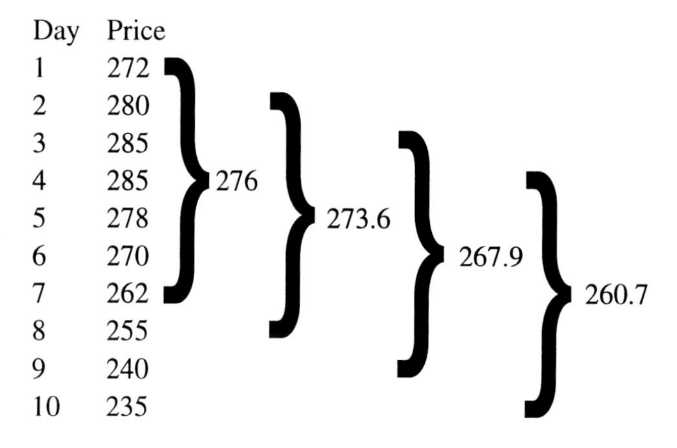

Moving averages can be calculated for any period to give you short, medium and long term views on the movement of a share price. The short term average can be obtained by taking a five day moving average (the number of working days in a week), the medium term by taking a 13 day average and a slightly longer term by taking a 20 day average. As the number of days in the moving average increases, then the moving average itself becomes smoother and less responsive to the short term fluctuations in the market. It is therefore slower to respond to changes in any trend and will give you fewer "false starts". However, as with all things, what you gain on the swings you lose on the roundabouts, and you will find that a large slice of the price move has already taken place by the time a longer moving average has singled a change.

It is possible to calculate other moving averages such as a "weighted" moving average where you give more significance to some data than to others. For example, you may wish to give the latest data in your set of prices more significance than the earlier data since it gives a better representation of current market thinking. A very crude way of achieving this would be to double the value of your last data point and then divide by the number of time periods plus one. A more effective and popular way with serious technical analysts is to use a weighting factor known as exponential smoothing. This gradually gives more and more significance to the latest data and therefore the latest information to enter the market. However you will certainly need a computer program to calculate an exponentially-smoothed moving average and full details of the exact technique are beyond the scope of this book.

The final point to address with moving averages is where you plot the "average point" that you calculated. Refer again to the seven day moving average that we calculated above. The first moving average data point of 276 refers to days 1-7. Now when you come to plot it on your chart, along with the actual price data, where do you place it? You basically have two main options:

- Either plot it against day four (the middle of your data), or
- Plot it on day seven (the end of your data) which is known as a "lagging" moving average.

Most technical analysts opt for the latter of these and plot the lagging moving average. Figure 6-1, below, shows a chart of price fluctuations for Glaxo Welcome shares along with a 20-day lagging moving average for the same data. Notice how peaks and troughs in the moving average data lag the same features in the actual price data.

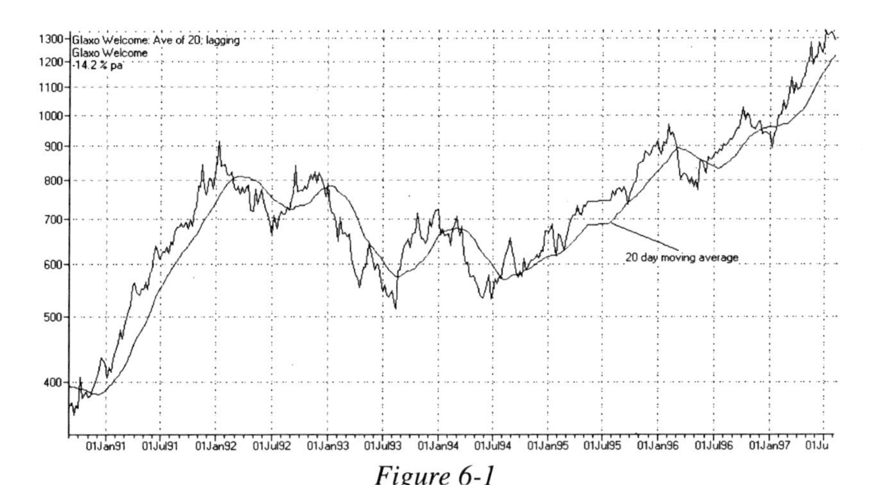

Figure 6-1

Interpreting the Moving Average

The simplest way to interpret a moving average line is to depict a change of direction as a signal to buy or sell. So a moving average which changes from the 'increasing' or 'level' to 'decreasing' is a signal to sell, and one which changes from 'decreasing' or 'level' to 'increasing' is a signal to buy. All you have achieved with this form of interpretation is a smoothing of the basic price data, and it does not really offer you much advantage.

The classical interpretation, which is used by most technical analysts, is to use a moving average curve in conjunction with the underlying price movements. Most investors typically:

- Buy when a share's price rises above its moving average, and
- Sell when the share's price falls below its moving average.

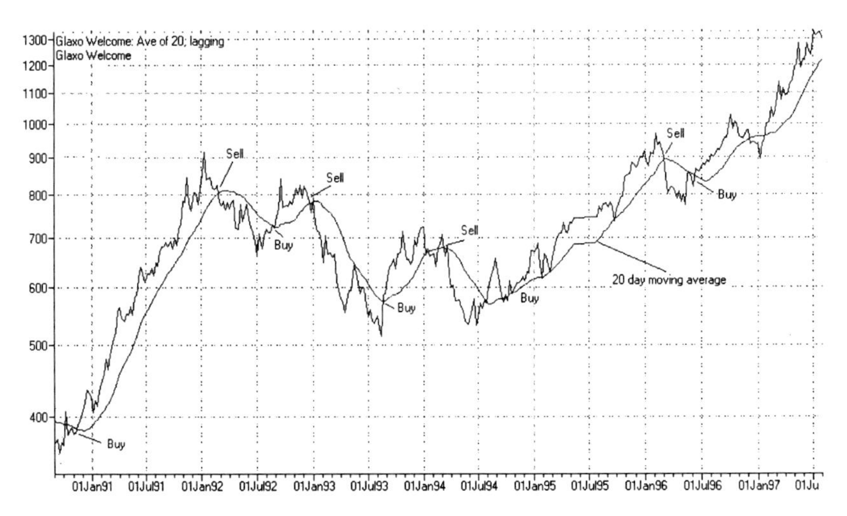

Figure 6-2 Buy and sell signals from the 20 day moving average of Glaxo Welcome shares.

Figure 6-2 again shows basic price data for Glaxo Welcome shares along with the 20 day moving average, lagging. But this time the buy and sell signals have been marked on. You can see that this is clearly a powerful system and one which can be recommended for any level of technical analyst.

Using such a system ensures that you will always be on the correct side of the market and, as indicated before, you will experience fewer false starts. Indeed, a price cannot rise too much without the underlying price rising above its average price. But the main disadvantage is that you will always tend to buy and sell late. You can see from Figure 6-2 that the actual point of the buy and sell signals is a day or two after the underlying price has started to fall or rise. On balance, my personal view is that the pros of using this system far out-weigh the cons. I would rather be on the right side of the market, and leave a bit of profit for others, than try to squeeze every single penny I can out of the market and end up taking a hit.

One last thing to note with this classical interpretation is that the change typically needs to last for a period around twice the length of the moving average for you to make money once dealing costs are taken into consideration.

Perhaps a more powerful way of interpreting the data but slightly more complex than the one moving average, is to combine a short term moving average and a longer term moving average on the same chart. Figure 6-3, overleaf, shows such a chart relating to shares in Cadbury Schweppes. Here you can see a five day moving average plotted alongside a 20 day moving average.

The normal interpretation is to sell when the short term moving average falls below the longer term moving average and to buy when it moves above. The buy and sell signals have been marked onto Figure 6-3 for clarification. The rational behind this interpretation is that the short term moving average (in this case five days) represents a "current" market consensus. The longer term moving average (in this case 20 days), on the other hand, represents the market consensus for

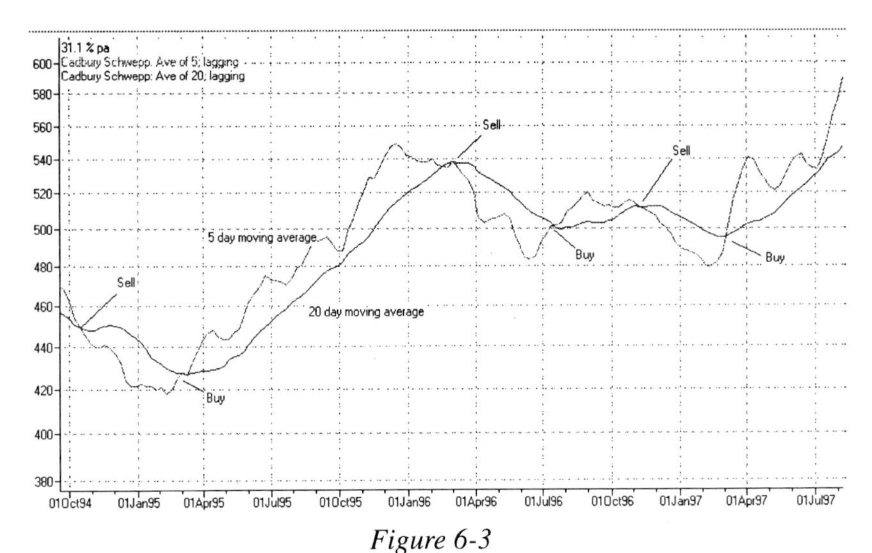

Figure 6-3
Long and short moving averages give good buy and sell signals

a period before the short term moving average. If the short term moving average is above the longer term moving average then "current" market expectations are for a higher share price. But if the longer term moving average is above the shorter term moving average then current market expectations are for a decreasing share price.

To show that this form of interpretation does, indeed, work I have taken Figure 6-3 and removed the moving averages but left on the buy and sell signals. Then I have plotted the underlying share price movements for Cadbury Schweppes shares to show that the signals did, indeed, work and would have produced a tidy profit (see Figure 6-4).

Three or more moving averages may be combined on the same chart to produce a far more complex system. These charts, however, tend to be a lot more difficult to interpret and produce many false starts. If you are an aggressive investor you find that you are making trades all the time and that very few of them are paying off, whilst less aggressive investors find that they will make very few trades and the ones they do make will last for a shorter duration. For both of these reasons I tend to leave them well alone.

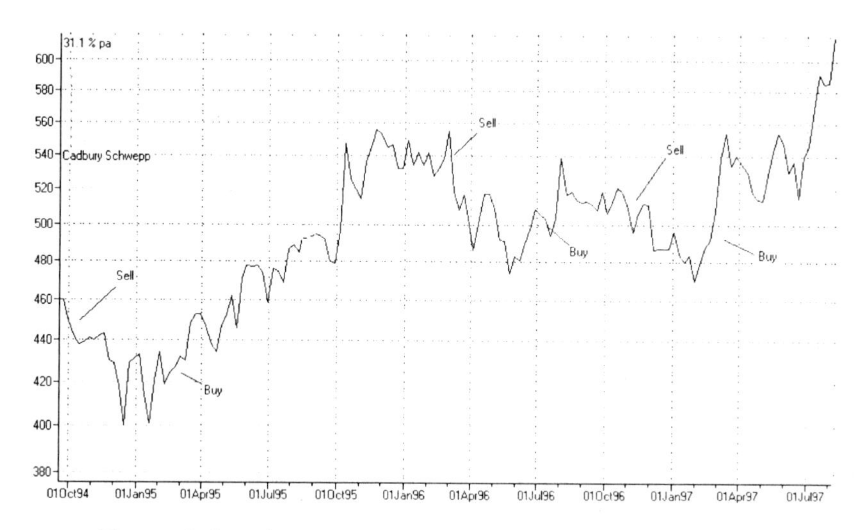

Figure 6-4 The same buy and sell signals (as Figure 6-3) superimposed on the real price data.

Smoothing Data

A side benefit of the moving average system is to smooth volatile data. If the value of a financial instrument tends to move wildly it can sometimes be difficult to see the underlying trends. So plotting a moving average curve instead of the basic price chart can sometimes give you a clearer view of what is going on. Figure 6-5 shows the data for Tomkins shares and a 20 day moving average plotted on a separate chart. You can see that the lower chart is easier to interpret and removes a lot of the noise which is apparent on the share price movement.

Figure 6-5

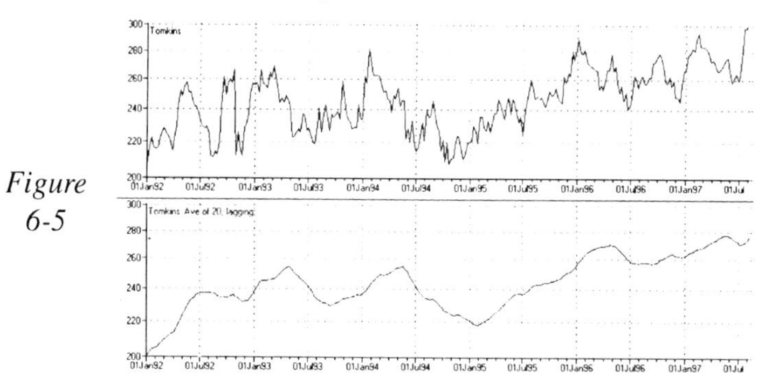

Chapter 7

Reversal Patterns

Whenever a price trend is in force, be it upwards or downwards, at some point it will come to an end. You could say there are actually three things that are certain in life:

Death, taxes and the end of trends!

The problem comes in predicting, exactly, when an uptrend or a downtrend or a sideways movement is going to come to an end. A technical analyst has many tools at his disposal to help him in his search for the end of a trend, but one of the most powerful is the presence of a **reversal pattern**.

These reversal patterns take the form of a characteristic shape on a chart and serve to give you an indication of which direction the market is going to move in, rather like patterns of stars were used by ancient mariners to navigate the seas. As you become more experienced in technical analysis you will learn to recognise the following patterns without a second thought:

- Head and shoulders top & bottom
- Double top & bottom
- Triple top & bottom
- Rounding top & bottom
- Broadening formation
- Rising and falling wedge

Head and Shoulders Top

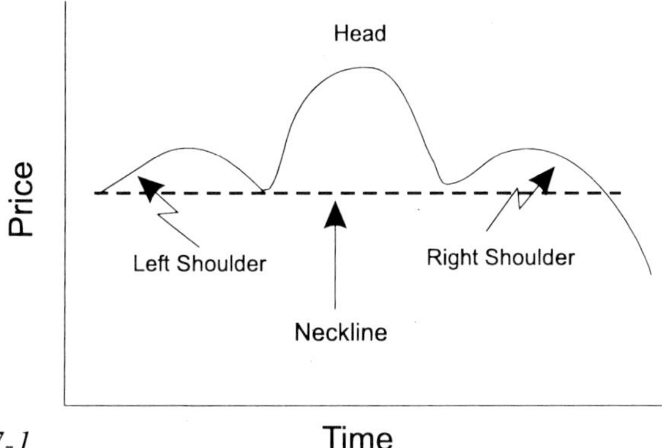

Figure 7-1

You will find that this formation is a common characteristic of many share price charts, and is one of the most reliable forms of reversal pattern. As its name implies, the shape consists of a left shoulder followed by a head and then a right shoulder.

The **left shoulder** is formed at the end of an extensive increase in price where the volume associated with it has been quite high. The shoulder rounds as the price dips slightly quite typically on lower volume. This dip is the start of the neck line and the head is about to form.

The **head** is then formed with associated heavy volume on the rising part of the head and less volume on the falling part. Prices then fall to somewhere near the same level as the low of the left shoulder. It does not have to be at exactly the same level and could be slightly higher or lower, but definitely below the top of the left shoulder.

All is set for the **right shoulder** to be formed by a rally in the price to a level roughly equal with that of the left shoulder. Again it can be slightly higher or lower but definitely below the high achieved by the head. The volume associated with this rally will usually be less than the rallies which formed the left shoulder and the head.

Once the right shoulder has started to form you can draw in a **neckline** across the bottoms created between the left shoulder and head and the head and right shoulder. Once the price falls from the right shoulder and breaks through the neckline the Head and Shoulders Top formation has been confirmed and it is your signal to go short in that particular financial instrument.

Quite often, once the neckline has been broken, you will see that prices will pull back towards the neckline before falling away sharply. This is similar to a "trader's remorse" period with the neckline acting as a resistance level instead of a mini support level during the Head and Shoulders Top formation. Keep a close eye on prices during this remorse period and be prepared to react in case it turns into a bull trap.

As indicated above, the Head and Shoulders Top formation does not need to be perfectly symmetrical. The time taken to create each of the shoulders may be different. This will cause one shoulder to look slightly larger than the other even though it has reached a similar high point. Also the neckline does not have to be exactly level and may slope up or down. This will make one of the shoulders look as though it is drooping or that the head is lopsided. Notice here, however, that it is important that the lowest point on the right shoulder must be lower than the highest point on the left shoulder, otherwise you may simply have an uptrend that is changing its gradient.

Head and Shoulders Bottom

This is quite obviously the opposite of a head and shoulders top! It usually accompanies a reversal from a downtrend to one which is in the upwards direction. The main difference between this and the Head and Shoulders Top is in the volume pattern associated with the share price movements. The volume should pick up as the prices increase from the bottom of the head and then increase even more on the rally which follows the right shoulder. If the neckline is broken with an associated low volume then you should be sceptical about the validity of the formation.

Double Top Formation

These appear in the shape of the letter 'M' on a chart and are also common.

A Double Top, believe it or not, is rather like a Head and Shoulder Top formation but without the head! A peak price is reached before a small decline, which causes the valley between the Double Tops, and then the price rallies again to a peak roughly equal to the level of the first. The price then falls away on a new downtrend.

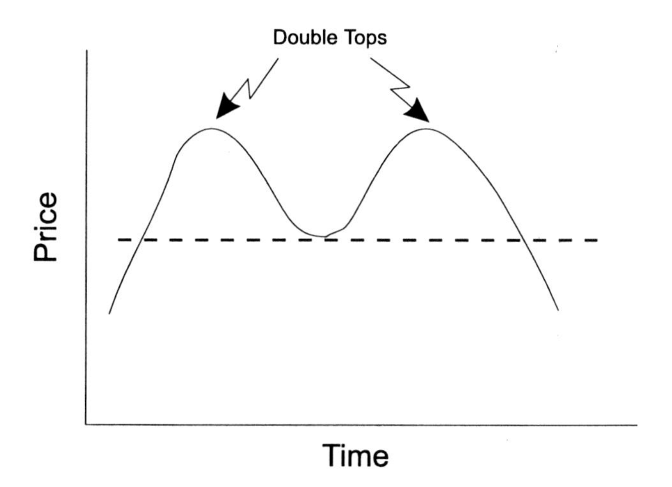

Figure 7-2 A classic Double Top reversal

The correct prediction of a true Double Top formation is more difficult than for a Head and Shoulder formation. This is because a simple uptrend, with each new wave of buying interspersed with minor reactions and profit taking, will appear as if it is making a

Double Top formation. However, as you can see in Figure 7-3, the data can progress in either direction.

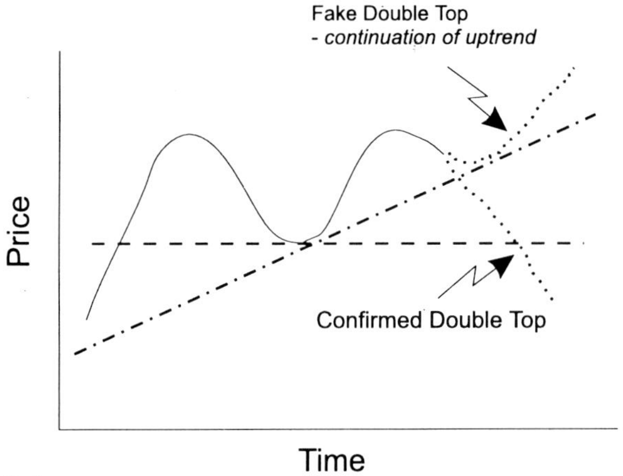

Figure 7-3

Once you reach the point shown by the end of the continuous line shown on Figure 7-3 you can not be sure if the Double Top formation will be confirmed and the price will drop away, or if the price will again rally and the uptrend will stay in force. In roughly 90% of cases you will find that the Double Top is, indeed, a fake in the making and the uptrend will stay in force.

Volume is, yet again, your best friend in determining whether a true Double Top formation is being created or if it is going to be a fake. Look at the volumes associated with both of the peaks. If the volume associated with the first peak is greater than that associated with the second peak then this is an indicator that the prices will fail to go higher - confirming the Double Top formation. If the volume accompanying the second rise is the same as that accompanying the first, or even greater, then it is likely that the uptrend will be continuing.

The time span taken to create the Double Top formation is another factor which can help you determine the likely progression of the price data. If the two tops are fairly close together in terms of time then you should suspect that it is merely a consolidation period, a pause for breath, before the rally continues. But if the peaks are separated over a longer period and the valley between the two peaks is fairly deep then you can be more sure that you are looking at a true Double Top.

Double Bottom

This is the opposite of a Double Top and appears as a letter 'W' on a chart. The formation of a double bottom and the indicators of the reversal are very much the same as for a Double Top. However the volume patterns are very different. This time a true double bottom formation will show increased volume on the rally up from the second bottom over the rally from the first bottom. If the volume associated with the rally from the second bottom is less than or equal to the volume associated with the rally from the first bottom, then you are probably looking at a pause in a continuing downtrend.

Triple Tops and Bottoms

These are a fairly rare species and you will not see them on many charts. As with the Head and Shoulders formation and the Double Top, the peaks and troughs do not have to be equally spaced. Nor do the peaks or the troughs have to reach the same levels or bottom out at exactly the same price to form a valid formation.

The volume associated with the Triple Top needs to be progressive. So the volume associated with the first peak needs to be larger than that associated with the second peak, which is itself larger than that associated with the third. Note, however, that the true Triple Top formation is not confirmed until prices have finally broken through a level equal with the lower of the two troughs.

A problem occurs, of course, with the Triple Top at the Double Top stage! Once the Double Top has been confirmed (in other words you realise that the uptrend is not continuing) it would be valid to think that the price is going to drop away sharply. However, the possibility remains that you are heading for a Triple Top. So a good trading strategy, if prices appear to be rallying slightly after a Double Top confirmation, is to go short in the market but to set a stop loss at a level equal to the highest peak of the Double Top formation.

Rounding Tops and Bottoms

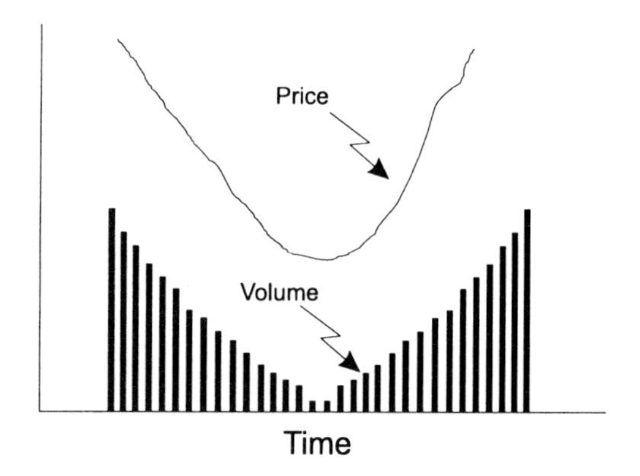

Figure 7-4

These appear to form an 'n' or 'u' shape on your chart and are hard to detect.

The way, yet again, to pick them out from a simple consolidation pattern is to look at the volume. In a true rounded bottom formation you will see that volume decreases as the price decreases, which signifies an easing of selling pressure. As the price movement becomes neutral and goes sideways you will see that there is very little trading activity and volumes are very low. Then, as prices start to increase, the volume will increase as well. The volumes and the prices, will now become almost a reflection of those which occurred during the decline.

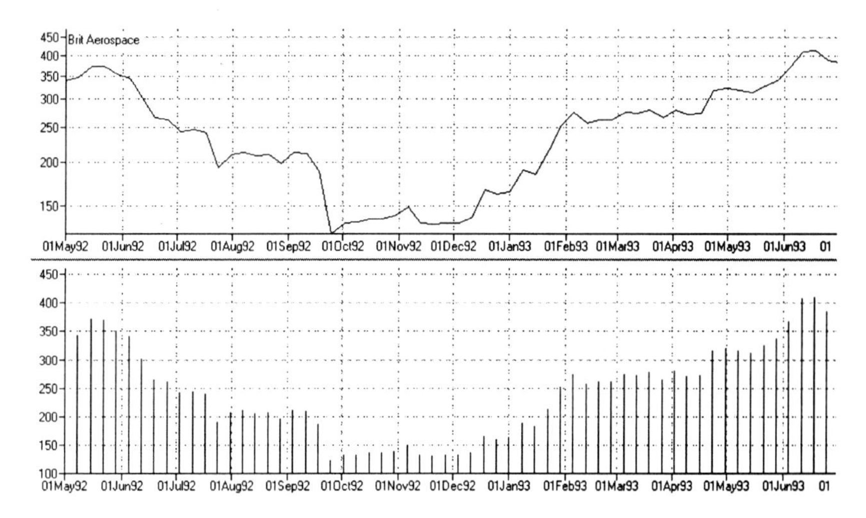

Figure 7-5 A rounded bottom at British Aerospace

Broadening Formations

The theory behind this reversal pattern is that five smaller reversals are followed by a substantial change. An example is shown in Figure 7-6 overleaf.

Note that "reversal" takes the literal meaning here and is a change of direction; so the five smaller reversals are changes from a falling market to a rising market, and a rising market to a falling market, and not five falls or five rises. Although the chart can be either way up, as a broadening tops or broadening bottoms reversal pattern, similar rules hold. Reversal three must occur at a higher level than reversal one, and reversal five, must be higher yet again. Also reversal four must occur at a lower level than reversal two (one, three and five must be successively lower, and two and four successively higher in the case of a broadening bottom).

The underlying idea behind this reversal pattern is that the market is almost out of control and lacking support from well-informed

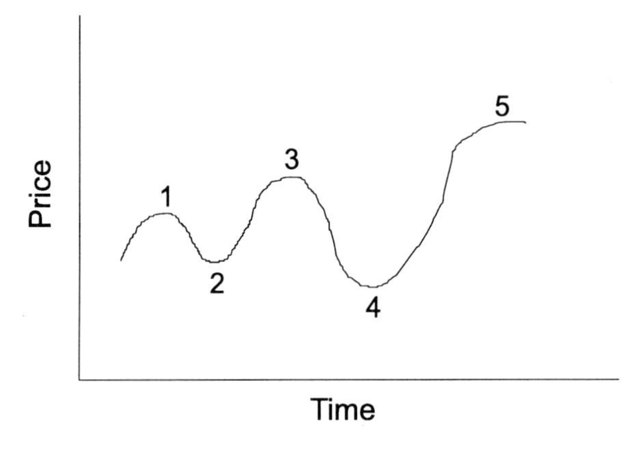

Figure 7-6

investors. The first reversal is supposedly created by "smart money" leaving the market, with the subsequent rises being attributed to an influx of the general public. Reversal number three is attributed to the smarter investors going short in stocks, whilst reversal five is, of course, the unavoidable drop. Volume is also erratic during this period and does not help with the interpretation of the charts.

Perhaps the best way to view this formation is as if the market is gradually becoming more and more unstable. As the swings get wilder and wilder something is going to break!

Wedge Formations

These can appear as rising or falling wedges. If you were to draw your trend lines along the bottoms of a share price movement and along the top, as per Chapter 4, instead of forming a parallel uptrend channel, they will converge to form a triangle. If the triangle is pointing upwards, as in Figure 7-7, then a market fall can be expected after the price curve penetrates the lower line. If the triangle is pointing downwards (a falling wedge) then the market will rise once the upper line is penetrated. If the wedge or triangle is level, in other words not pointing up or down, then this is a "consolidation" pattern and you can expect the trends to continue.

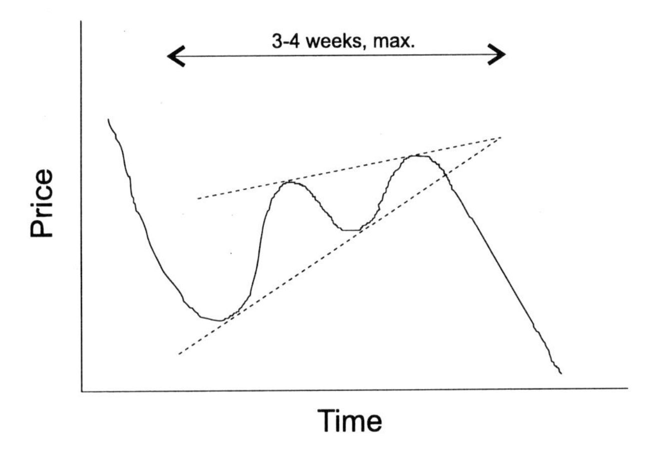

Figure 7-7.

You will notice on Figure 7-7 that a time period of 3-4 weeks across the entire formation has been marked. This is because wedge formations only occur as reversals of intermediate and minor trends. They will not be seen, except in unusual circumstances, as a reversal to a major market trend.

Chapter 8

Indicators and Oscillators

In its simplest form, an indicator is an arithmetical calculation made on the basis of fluctuations in the price of a financial instrument and/or the volume associated with it. The resultant value is then used to predict future changes in prices. In other words it is giving an **indication** of what is to come.

An **oscillator** is very similar to an **indicator** in that it predicts future changes in the price movement of a financial instrument. However an oscillator should strictly be "normalised". This means that all values are changed so that they fall between +1 and -1, or alternatively +100% and -100%. This is achieved by taking the indicator and dividing all of the available data by the maximum possible value. To see how this works, let's look at the momentum indicator.

Momentum

The basic **momentum indicator** is one of the simplest technical analysis equations available. It is a calculation of the difference between the current market price of an instrument and the price of the same instrument a certain number of days ago.

The momentum indicator = (current value - value N days ago)

The number of days, N, will depend on your interest in the market. If you are a regular trader then you will use a low value for N, but if you are building a pension portfolio then you will use a large value for N.

To use this momentum indicator in its raw form you would simply buy the financial instrument when the indicator becomes positive and sell when it turns negative. In other words you are buying when the price is picking up momentum and selling when that momentum has been lost. Again, like many other analysis tools in this book, it is a lagging technique and you will enter the market after it has made a turn or reversal. But although you will miss the beginning of the change you should be able to participate in the main action.

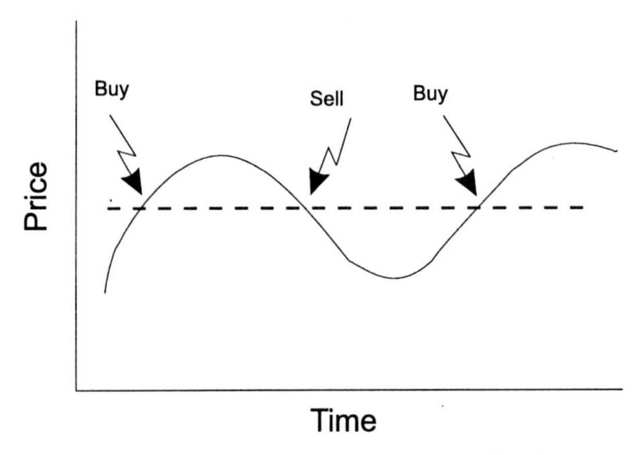

Figure 8-1 Price momentum indicator

To convert the momentum indicator into a true oscillator you now need to divide by the maximum obtainable momentum value. Some markets such as the commodity markets and the American T-Bill market set a limit on the maximum change allowed in one day. This gives you an obvious figure with which to divide your momentum indicator. However most markets do not operate in this manner. Instead you need to set an arbitrary limit which will give you a general idea of price movement in your expected time frame.

Such a limit, for the ordinary investor, could be a period of one year. Look back over the price fluctuations for the last 12 months and calculate the momentum indicator throughout the year. Then run through the resultant data and find the maximum and minimum momentum indicator that you have calculated. Finally, to calculate your momentum oscillator, divide all the data you have calculated for the year by the larger of the maximum or minimum. You will now be able to plot your **momentum oscillator** and see that, although it has the same shape as the momentum indicator, the scales are easier to understand.

You now use this new chart to calculate when a market is "overbought" or "oversold". In an **overbought market** virtually all the investors who had intended buying a particular financial instrument have already committed the money that they are using to invest. Any further influx of money in favour of that instrument is possibly coming from short term speculators or less informed investors who are simply jumping on the band wagon. Naturally an **oversold market** is one in which the smart money has already switched out or gone short and any further price drop can also be attributed to the "me too" syndrome.

Exactly when the momentum oscillator indicates that the market for a financial instrument is overbought or oversold is almost as arbitrary as setting out the maximum and minimum indicator levels or the value for N in your original momentum calculation. Remember, technical analysis, as we have said before, is as much an art as a science. The answer lies in whether your aim is to lag or to lead the market.

If you are quite happy to enter a market once a change has already taken place and simply profit from the majority of a price change, then you will be quite happy to use a momentum indicator (or any other indicator) to trade with the trend. In other words you will use the oscillator to buy and sell whenever it crosses the zero line and make your move according to its direction.

If your aim is to beat the market you will be intending to make your move before a new trend takes hold. In this situation you are looking to make your trades when the momentum oscillator is at a peak or a trough. Obviously you do not know when this is going to occur be-

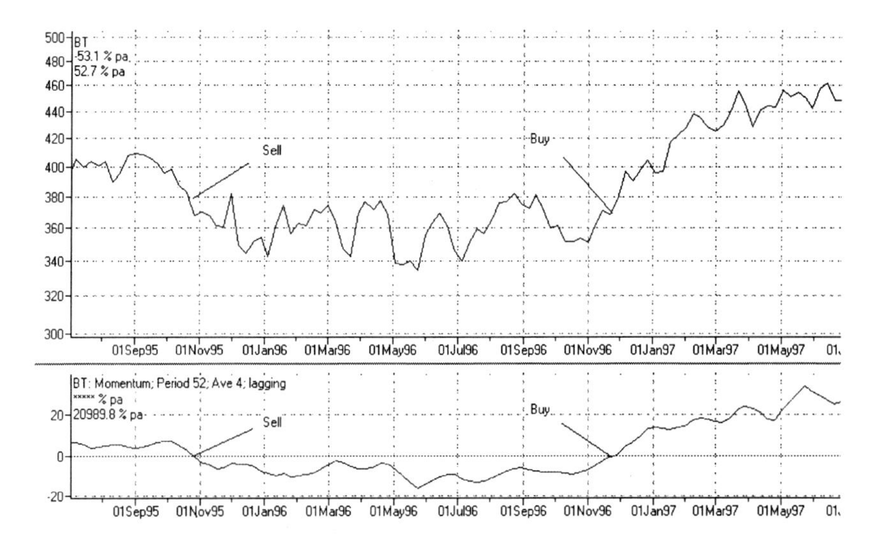

Figure 8-2 Using the Momentum Indicator to buy and sell BT shares

cause the oscillator does not always reach right up to +1 or -1. So, instead, you should aim to make your trades when the oscillator reaches, say, 0.8 or above. With such a strategy you will be going against the short-term trend and essentially taking a punt on the chances of a technical reaction occurring.

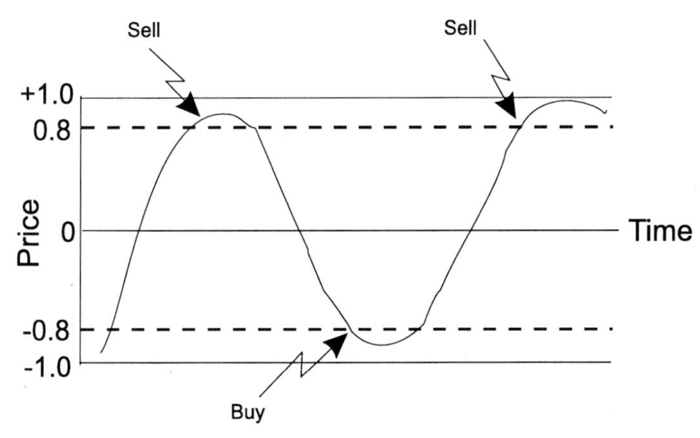

Figure 8-3
Buying and selling ahead of the market using the Momentum Oscillator

Rate of Change

The Rate of Change indicator (ROC) is a way of showing how rapidly the price of a particular financial instrument is moving. The underlying principle is that if a price is rising (or falling) very quickly there will soon come a time when it is thought to be overbought (or oversold). When this occurs the price may still continue to rise (or fall), but not as rapidly as it was before.

This oscillator always has a value between zero and 10 and is calculated from the average of all price rises in a given period divided by the average of all price falls in the same period. Again the choice of period is arbitrary and dependent on your position in the markets.

The rate of change indicator is:

$$ROC = 100 - 100/(1+X)$$

where:

$$X = (\text{average of price rises}) / (\text{average of price falls})$$

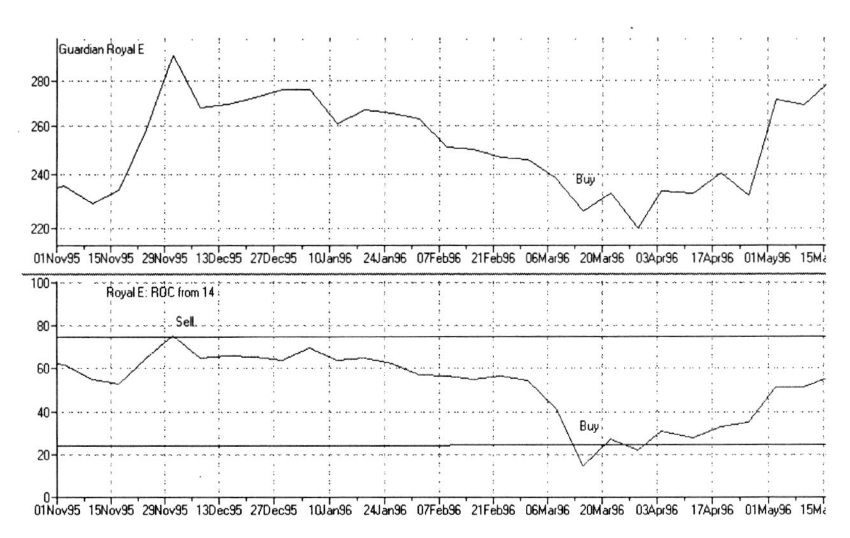

Figure 8-4

Selling and then buying signals from the Rate of Change oscillator

The neutral position of this oscillator is at 50; if it rises above then the instrument is becoming overbought, if it falls below it is becoming oversold. Critical levels exist at 75 and 25. An ROC above or below these levels indicate the instrument is very overbought or very oversold, and a price reversal is considered extremely imminent.

Price Minus Average

If you take a price chart and superimpose the moving average over top you will see the price is sometimes above the average and at other times below. The Price Minus Average is simply the difference between the two curves. So when the price and moving average curves cross one another the Price Minus Average oscillator will be at the value zero, when the price is above the average it will be positive and when the price is below the average it will be negative.

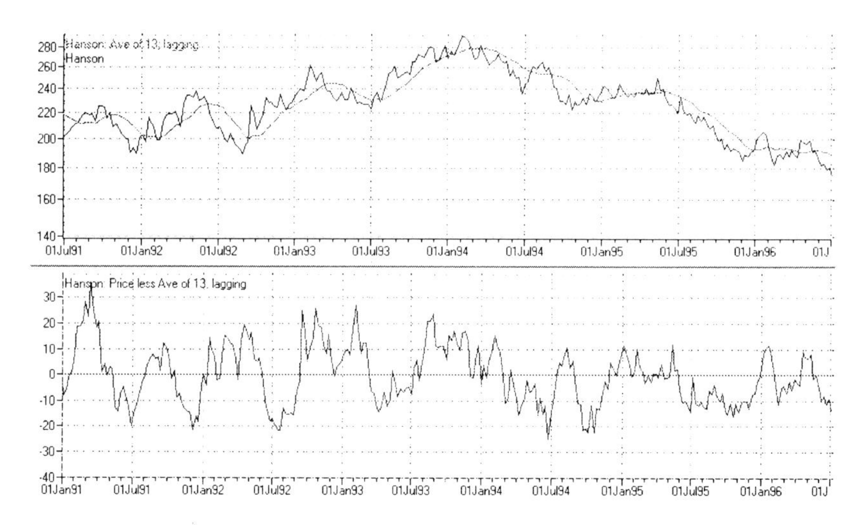

Figure 8-5 Price Minus Average oscillator for Hanson shares

This oscillator allows you to see clearly how big the difference is between the current price and a long term average Figure. To obtain buy and sell signals, follow the same routine as you did with the momentum indicator and divide your data by the larger of the maximum or minimum obtained over a certain period. You can then set your buy and sell signals when the curve crosses the zero line (lagging the market) or at a high percentage of the normalised value such as 0.8 or 0.9 (leading the market).

The Relative Strength Index (RSI)

This oscillates between an upper limit of 100 and a lower limit of zero. If the RSI is above 70 then the market is thought to be overbought and the forecast is for a fall. If the RSI is below 30 then the market is thought to be oversold and the forecast is for a rise.

You calculate the relative strength index by;

$$\text{RSI} = 100 - \left(\frac{100}{\sum (+\text{ changes} / -\text{ changes}) + 1} \right)$$

Moving Average Convergence/ Divergence (MACD)

This is a simple modification of the average chart to show divergence (or convergence) of two separate moving averages. One of these moving averages will be calculated for the short term and one for a longer term. When the instrument is trending in one direction, say upwards, the shorter term moving average will rise quicker than the longer term moving average.

The difference between these two averages is calculated and then normalised in the usual manner. As the MACD falls below or rises above the zero line it forecasts that the instrument will fall or rise corresponding as supply/demand lines move up and down inline with investor expectations. The further the MACD moves from the benchmark zero line, the stronger the trend is likely to be.

A variation used on the MACD by many analysts is known as the **signal line**. This is used to help you lead the market and anticipate the convergence of the two moving averages. Plot your MACD in the usual way and then superimpose a moving average of the MACD itself (not of the underlying financial instrument price). You should buy when the MACD moves above the signal line and sell when it moves below.

Volume Accumulation Indicator

This technical indicator was created by Marc Chaikin and it measures trading volume in relation to price fluctuations. It works on the hypothesis that if a market spends most of the day on a downward trend, but ends on a positive note, the positive trend should be interpreted in relation to the whole which was largely negative.

So, the Volume Accumulation Formula looks like this;

$$VA= [((MC-ML) - (MH-MC)) / (MH-ML)] \times V$$

where VA is volume accumulation, MC is the market close, ML is the market low, MH is the market high and V is the volume.

The volume accumulator line can now be compared to the basic price line and you should look for divergences between the two trends. For example, if the volume accumulator line fails to confirm an upward price trend (divergence of the two lines), a fall in the underlying instrument price is being indicated.

Chapter 9

Market Indicators

All the charts and indicators that you have looked at so far are used to calculate the movement of specific financial instruments such as shares, commodities, or options. But there are another set of technical analysis tools which are used to analyse groups of instruments within a market or whole markets themselves. Not surprisingly these indicators are usually referred to as "market indicators".

One of the benefits of looking to the whole market is the amount of data that is available. For a particular financial instrument you are usually limited to the opening closing high and low prices plus volume. Whereas for overall markets you get extra data such as the number of instruments that have reached a new high during the day, the number of instruments that have increased in price and a comparison of the volume associated with increased price.

Why should you look at the market as a whole when you wish to buy individual financial instruments? The answer lies in the overall concept of financial risk. When you go into a market and purchase a specific financial instrument you are taking on two forms of risk: **Specific Risk** and **Market Risk**.

Specific Risk is unique to the instrument that you are taking on, whilst the Market Risk refers to the whole market in which the specific instrument is traded. For example, if you purchase an oil stock such as British Petroleum you run the risk that they can announce worse than expected profits or a decrease in their oil reserves. But you also take on the risk associated with the entire oil sector which could include OPEC countries opening the taps or another Middle East flare up. So, in short, it is much less risky purchasing a single financial instrument when you know the direction in which the market as a whole is moving.

Market Indicator Categories

Market indicators fall into one of three categories: momentum, monetary and sentiment.

Momentum indicators look at what prices are actually doing and include all of the price/volume indicators which have previously been discussed (but applied to the markets instead of individual instruments), the number of instruments that have broken new highs versus those that have recorded new lows, and the relationship between the number of instruments that have increased in price compared to those which have fallen.

Monetary indicators are those such as interest rates, money supply, debt and inflation.

Sentiment indicators look at investor expectations for the whole market. Often these are discernible from price movements themselves but also include indicators such as the put/call ratio, and the ratio of bulls to bears.

Market Momentum

The **advance-decline** line is, perhaps, the most important indicator of the state of the stock market. It is calculated by taking the number of instruments that have improved and subtracting the number that have declined during the day. The result is then added or subtracted accordingly, each day, to an accumulative number. This new aggregate is then plotted on a line chart.

The advance-decline line then gives you an indication as to whether the market as whole is gaining or losing strength over the days. Because it is a measure of the number of stocks, and not based on capitalisation, it often signals the end of a trend in a market before any of the averages. So, the Footsie may be increasing and the advance-decline line decreasing. This means that even though the market average is up the majority of other stocks are declining, which is a warning that the bull market is deteriorating and a fall is signalled. Similarly if the Footsie was falling and the advance-decline line increasing, then you could expect the Footsie to do an about turn and start on an uptrend.

Again the theory behind this is propped up by the fact that knowledgeable investors are always the first to invest in a rising market and the first to get out when a market stops rising. So, while the majority of less informed investors are concentrating on the headline stocks, those in the "know" are liquidating their positions across the market.

As you delve into the advance-decline indicator you will find that there is a sensitivity that depends on which phase the market is in (from The Dow Theory) and whether the market is near a top or a bottom. The following table summarises these minor differences:

FTSE	Advance-Decline Line	Prediction
Rising Prices	Falling	Falling
Near Previous Top	Below Corresponding Top	Falling
Near Previous Top	Above Corresponding Top	Still Rising
Falling	Rising	Rising
Near Previous Bottom	Above Previous Bottom	Rising
Near Previous Bottom	Below Previous Bottom	Falling

Unchanged Stocks

Another useful indicator as to the momentum of the market lies not in the number of shares that are increasing or falling but in the number that remain unchanged. The theory dictates that when more stocks than normal remain unchanged in price the market as a whole is about to change direction, meaning a top or a bottom. To calculate the unchanged shares index divide the number of stocks that remained unchanged by the total number that are traded. You will find that the resultant percentage is usually between 5 and 25%. If the unchanged shares index is near to the 5% level then this is considered a bullish signal, but an index near the 25% level is thought of as being bearish.

Market Sentiment

Market sentiment indicators attempt to judge the mood of investors and how they think the market is going to unfold. Most centre around the activities of various participants in the market. A sharp division is perceived between the **market professionals** (which include market makers, brokers and exchange members) and the **general public** (you and I). Whilst the perception may not be *entirely* correct the general public are thought of as "unsophisticated" investors i.e:

The professionals believe that the public get everything wrong!

So they keep as much an eye on who is trading as what is being traded.

The Americans often refer to "**odd-lot**" purchases and sales. These refer to transactions which involve a low number of shares or are below a certain value (say, less than 1000 shares or £5,000 worth). The belief is that these purchases and sales must originate from the general public and represent less sophisticated activity. And, since the general public get everything wrong, a large volume of "odd-lot" buying is an indicator that the market is about to fall. Similarly increased "odd-lot" selling, the theory goes, is a sure fire indicator that the markets are about to rise. At this point, it has to be said that there is a certain amount of truth in these beliefs. Whenever news of a market fall hits the airwaves or appears in a Sunday newspaper there is quite a lot of panic selling and often centred around the "popular" shares such as the privatised utilities and recently floated building societies. Also, when the market is getting frothy, there is a certain amount of "me too" syndrome that creeps in and people who would not normally buy shares throw their hard earned cash into the market without realising the full risk.

Other indicators and ratios are calculated by looking at purchases and sales made by the so called professionals. These are supposed to be indicators of where the "smart money" is going and, of course, the theory is that you should follow it. **Members of a stock exchange** would fall into this category and various ratios are calculated by looking at the number of shares bought or sold by members compared to the total volume traded in the same period.

At this point you may be asking yourself why you haven't been given the exact method for calculating these "odd-lot" and "specialist" indicators and ratios. Well, the simple answer is that you would not be able to make use of the information. The data that you require is simply not readily available to the ordinary investor.

Of course if you are a member of a stock exchange or if you subscribe to a specialist service you will be able to get hold of the information that you require and calculate any number of indicators that you wish. However if you fall into this sort of category then you are already considered "smart money" and should know what you are doing. This, of course, raises a question as to why the smart money requires a signal to tell it what to do!

Bull/Bear Ratio

A more accessible indicator to market sentiment for the ordinary investor is known as the **Bull/Bear ratio**. It is supposedly common knowledge that stock market investment advisers, whichever investment house they come from, are trend followers as opposed to market leaders. So when the market is rising they are bullish and when it is falling they are bearish. Indeed, they often go over the top and tend to be far too optimistic in a rising market and overly pessimistic in a falling market.

This information can be used to give you an indicator of when a reversal is likely to take place. High readings of the Bull/Bear ratio are themselves bearish since it is considered that there are too many bulls amongst the advisers. And low readings are considered bullish since there are not enough bulls amongst the advisers. It sounds such a simple ratio to calculate (if you can find out the true feelings of the various analysts) but it has given remarkably good indicators over the long term. Historically values of over 60% for the bull/bear ratio have been enough to indicate "extreme" optimism and the onset of a bearish market. Whereas readings of below 40% for the Bull/Bear ratio have been sufficient to indicate extreme pessimism and time for a bullish market.

Put/Call Ratio

Puts and Calls are the names given to share options which are traded on the *London International Financial Futures and Options Exchange* (LIFFE).

The holder of a **call option** has the right to buy a certain number of shares in a specified company at a fixed price on a specific day. Note that, as the name suggests, the holder has the option or the right to buy, not an obligation. The number of shares involved depends on how many option contracts have been purchased, with one contract being for 1,000 shares. The right to buy these shares obviously has a value and that is the price of the call option contract.

Holders of **put options** have the right to sell a certain number of shares in a specific company at a set price on a specific day. As before, it is an option and not an obligation.

Options are known as "wasting assets" because, as the exercise date approaches, their value tends towards zero. Also they provide a high degree of **gearing** with a relatively small investment potentially offering huge rewards and the danger of equally large losses. As a consequence they tend to be traded by sophisticated investors who are speculating on the market and by professionals who may be hedging the risks involved with other financial instruments. For more information see my book on ***Understanding Financial Risk in a Day*** also published by Take That Limited (details on page 96).

Purchasers of Puts obviously expect the market to decline whereas purchaser of Calls expect the market to rise. So the relationship between the number of Puts to Calls give an indication of the relationship between bearish and bullish expectations. So, as option traders become bearish as a group, the put/call ratio will increase, and as they become bullish as a group the put/call ratio will decline.

Monetary Indicators

These indicators generally give you a feeling for how much money is swilling about in "the system" and therefore available for investment. No single one of these indicators can give you pointers as to where the markets are heading, but taken as a whole they can certainly help with your investment decision.

Money Supply

There are five measures of money supply within the UK known as M0, M1, M2, M3 and, imaginatively, M4.

The first, M0, is a measure of the value of notes and coins in circulation plus banker's working balances. M1 is a measure of how much money is available to be spent immediately. It includes M0 plus cheque accounts and all other instant access accounts. M2 includes all of the M1 supply plus assets which are invested for the short term. The short term investments include money market accounts and money market mutual funds. The fourth, M3, includes all of M1 plus M2 plus larger deposits. These larger deposits include institutional money market funds and agreements between banks. M4 is the widest measure of money supply.

The **growth in M1 money supply** gives technical analysts the best indication of any forthcoming changes in the stock market. The greater the increase in M1 money supply the greater the chance of an upturn in the market.

Net Free Reserves

These are a measure of the liquidity in the banking system. It represents the **excess cash that banks are holding in their reserves** over and above their legal requirements. If banks have "net free reserves" they have more money than they 'need' and are therefore able to lend that money to businesses. This, in turn, funds business growth and economic expansion leading to gains on a stock market.

When banks are short on cash and are at or below their legal requirements they are said to have "net borrowed reserves". This means that they have few funds available for lending to business; leading to lower growth and, perhaps, falls in the market.

Interest Rates

The interest rate set by the Bank of England is known as the **base rate** and it creates a level from which all other interest rates are calculated.

As you will no doubt be aware it is a hot media topic because of the direct influence it has on everyone in the country. If base rates go up the cost of your mortgage will increase and you will pay more interest on any other borrowings such as credit card purchases. However it is the effects on business that are of more interest to the technical analyst. Virtually all businesses have huge borrowings and so an increase in base rates will directly affect their bottom line. Less money will be available for dividend payments, making shares less attractive and therefore worth less money than if interest rates were lower.

So, as a general rule of thumb, a fall in base rates can be viewed as a bullish indicator for the stock market, and an increase in base rate would be considered bearish.

It should be noted, however, that interest rates are changing far more frequently than they have done historically. This means that any bad or good news is drip fed into the market and there are less surprises around the corner. Politicians and bankers are also acutely aware of the influence that interest rates have on consumer sentiment as well as business sentiment and so they take more care when setting base rates. This means that interest rate changes on their own are now not enough to knock a market out of its stride.

Chapter 10

Cycles

We are very used to many cycles affecting our daily lives. Our basic time frame is split into cycles; every 60 seconds we complete a minute, every 60 minutes we complete an hour, every 24 hours we complete a day, and every 365 days we complete a year. These are not arbitrary functions but they have their basis in nature. The length of days is dictated by the rate at which the Earth rotates and the year is set by how long it takes for our planet to orbit the sun. Then the combination of the Earth's distance from the sun, the solar orbit and its rotation gives us another set of cycles with the seasons: Spring, Summer, Autumn and Winter.

The way in which nature exerts its influence over the financial markets is most noticeable in the commodities markets. Think about a typical year. First the markets try to anticipate how much of a crop will be made from the planting intentions of suppliers. Then there is concern about the weather patterns during the growing season. And then there is relief or concern over the size of the harvest. Since there aren't many crops that can be harvested at any time of the year, the concerns associated with each step of the growing cycle occur at roughly the same time every year.

But it is not just in the commodity market that seasonal patterns are recognisable. Think for a moment about the hotel and leisure sector. In this country most people tend to go on holiday during the summer months. So it is at the same time every year that hotels experience their highest occupancy levels. Similarly airlines will be transporting more people during the same period every year. And when did you book your last summer holiday, paying the deposit and boosting the holiday company's cashflow? Chances are it was early in the new year.

That brings up another cycle that has a very big influence on many industries - public holidays. The output of many industries and sectors are targeted towards one time of the year such as Christmas. Publishers of books on humour may only sell a few copies of each book during the year but at Christmas their sales will soar. Also consider manufacturers of fireworks - their entire output is virtually consumed in one day!

Although the seasons have by far the biggest influence on our lives, not all cycles repeat themselves every 12 months. Some cycles are extremely short in duration such as the arrival of our pay packet (hopefully). Most people get paid every week, which exhibits itself as a mini boom in spending on a Friday night and a Saturday afternoon. Other cycles could be of a longer duration. For example how often do you change your car? Most people tend to keep a car for 2-3 years and then trade it in for a newer model.

Whatever forces govern the cycles in our lives the fact exists that the financial markets also exhibit cyclical movement. Chartists have found cycles in the financial markets with frequencies ranging from minutes to tens of years. Most of these, of course, are totally useless to the average technical analyst. But the medium and longer term cycles are critical to the amount of money that you can make.

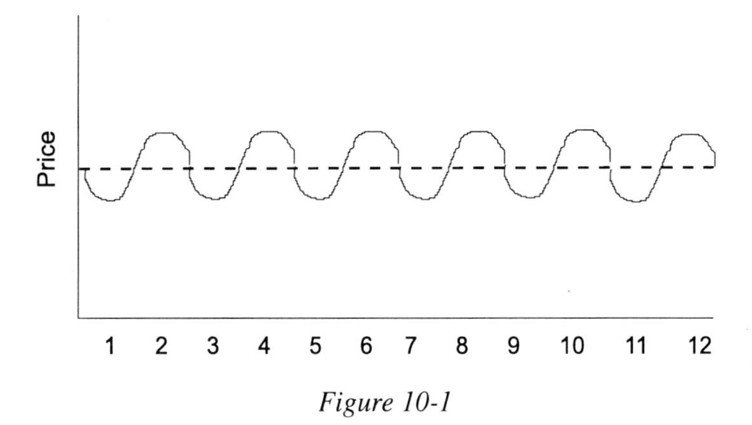

Figure 10-1

Consider the hypothetical share price movement shown in Figure 10-1. A long term **investor** who bought at the beginning of the year and sold at the end would show zero profit if dealing costs are ignored. But a short term investor, or **trader**, who traded the cycles and religiously bought at the start of odd numbered months and sold at the start of even numbered months would have accumulated a handy profit.

Even if the share price movement shown in Figure 10-1 had been part of a major uptrend line (shown in Figure 10-2) the trader would have shown more profit at the end of the year than the longer term investor.

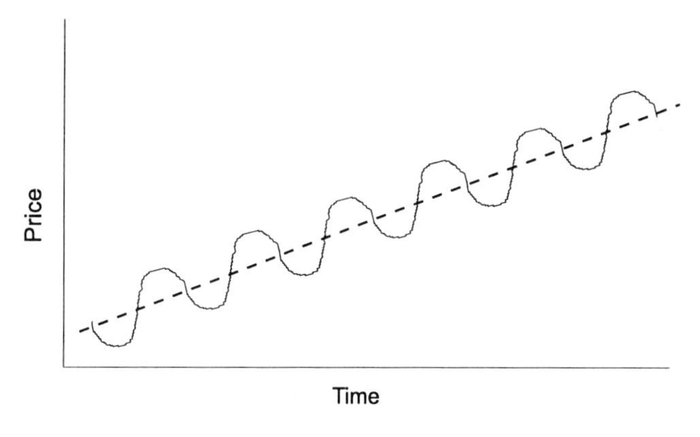

Figure 10-2

If the trader had also compounded his profits during the year by investing his entire capital to date at the start of each even month (original investment plus profit) then his "extra profit " would have been even greater.

Use of Cycles

The first step in making good use of cycles in the stock market is to select a few, but not too many, stocks that show reasonable volatility over short periods. Figure 10-3 shows a definition of magnitude and period as related to cycles on a chart. The shares that you select must have a reasonable magnitude so that you can make a profit once dealing costs have been taken into consideration.

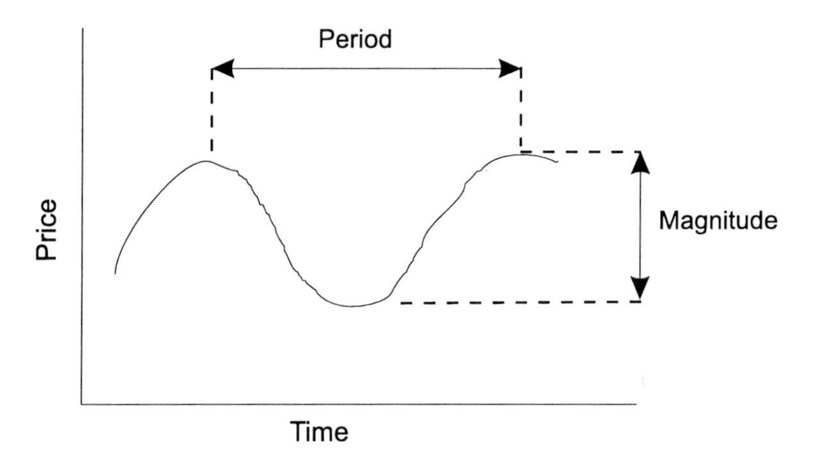

Figure 10-3

Once you have chosen the shares that you wish to work on, make a chart of the fluctuations in price over any period. Then identify tops or bottoms during that period. You will need to find five or six reasonably distinct features for the technique to work. Now measure in terms of time, the period between each top (or bottom). Finally, calculate the average period over the time covered by your chart.

You have now calculated the time that it usually takes for your share to go through one price cycle. So if your share is already at a peak, it should peak again after the period that you have just calculated.

An important factor to bear in mind is that the markets are not perfect. If they were we would all be millionaires by the end of the year! Instead, you will find that there are small discrepancies in the regularity of the cycles. So it is usual for analysts to allow a 10% error in both directions. In other words, if you are at a peak, the next peak could occur anywhere between *0.9 x (your estimated period)* and *1.1 x (your estimated period).*

Remember that cycles occur with different frequencies. So a cycle with a lower frequency will be superimposed on top of one with a longer frequency. In other words a major uptrend or downtrend may be part of a very long term cycle, and smaller cycles will occur within this larger cycle. If you look at Figure 10-4 you will see how the imposition of a short term cycle on top of a trend will form an apparent uptrend channel.

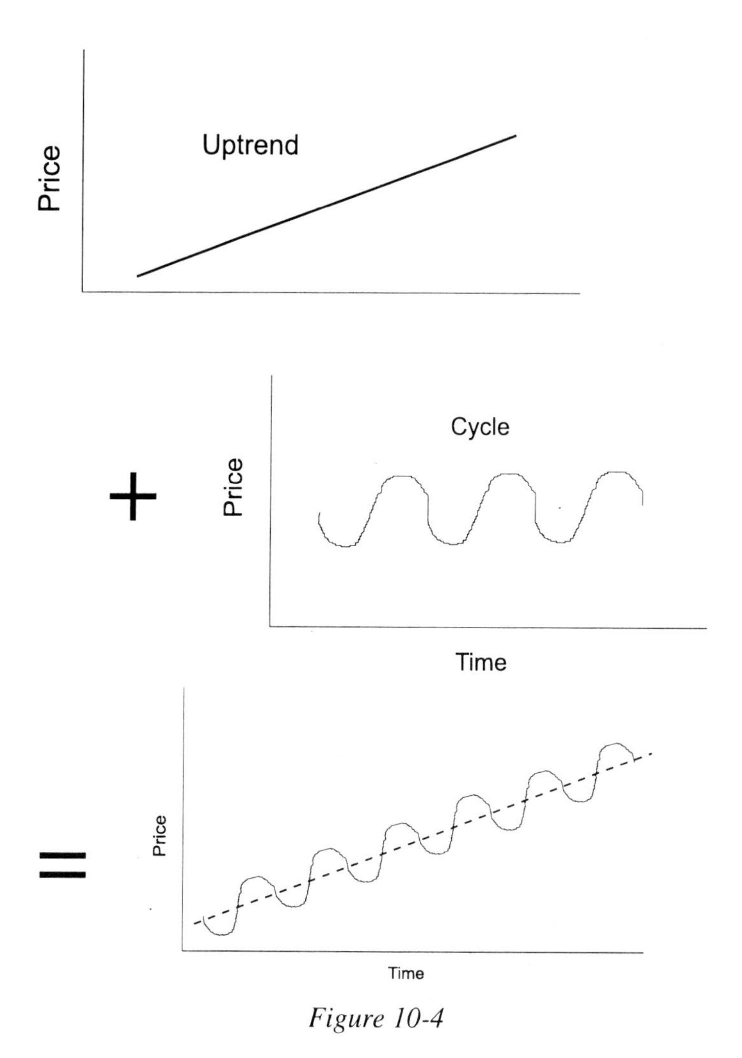

Figure 10-4

Nearly every chart can be broken down in this way with very high frequency cycles superimposed on top of medium term cycles which themselves are all superimposed on top of long term cycles. And, if buy now you are becoming a little sceptical, here's a real life example of medium term cycles (trough to trough) superimposed on a major uptrend for the FTSE-100 index during 1996 and the start of 1997. So you can see the cycles a little easier I have taken the moving average of 5 days instead of the actual index; this short-term moving average gets rid of the noise without losing any of the background trends.

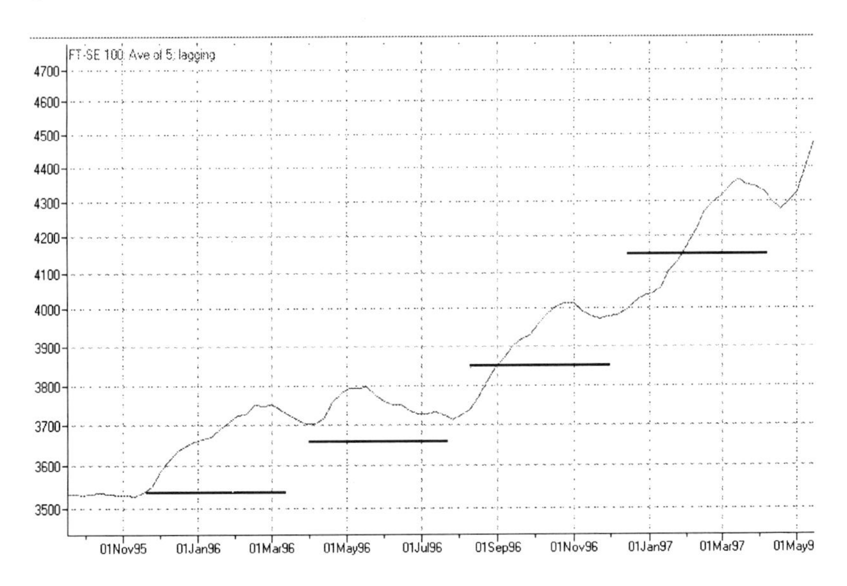

Figure 10-5 Cycles in the FTSE-100 index.

Advanced Cycle Theory

The **Elliott Wave** theory was developed by Ralph Nelson Elliott in a series of articles published in Financial World magazine in 1939 and 1940. Elliott believed that all of mankind's activities are characterised by an identifiable series of waves. He applied this to all forms of social activities including the stock market.

The basic concepts behind the Elliott Wave theory can be listed in three statements:

1. Mankind's activities are characterised by waves,
2. Those waves form patterns which reoccur, and
3. Action is followed by reaction.

Taking the theory a little further, Elliott suggested some very specific characteristics:

- There are five waves in the direction of the main trend followed by three corrective waves in the opposite direction.
- Those **five waves and three corrective waves complete one full cycle**. This cycle then becomes two "sub-divisions" of the next "bigger" five-three wave.
- The underlying five-three pattern remains constant even though the time period for each cycle may vary.

In other words Elliott Wave theory is suggesting that a five-three wave count forms a small cycle. That cycle is then part of a Supercycle. In turn the Supercycle is part of a Grand Supercycle. And, moving in the other direction, cycles can be broken down into their own five-three components of primary, intermediate, minute and sub-minute cycles.

Figure 10-6 overleaf shows how an ideal Elliott Wave theory cycle looks like a jerky, sore tooth pattern rather than a simple, smooth up or downtrend.

The complete Elliottt Wave theory is even more complex than this with other wave cycles being created in line with the Fibonacci sequence. Each of Elliott's cycles consist of a wave count that falls within the Fibonacci sequence.

Leonardo Fibonacci was a twelfth century mathematician who discovered a sequence of numbers within intriguing relationships. The sequence is

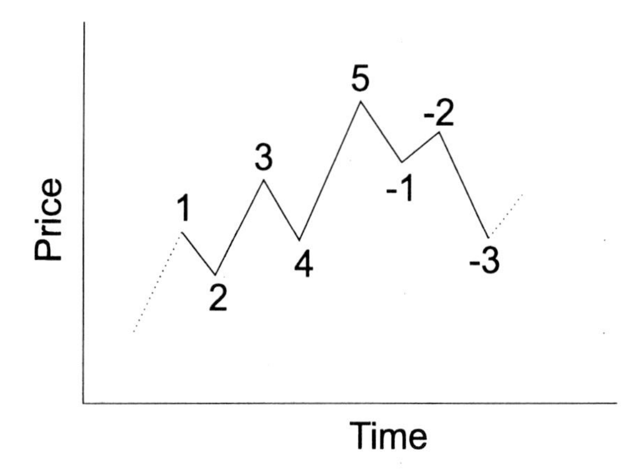

Figure 10-6

created by starting with the number one and simply adding the number that precedes it to create the next number in the sequence. So 1+0=1, 1+1=2, 2+1=3, 3+2=5, 5+3=8, etc. The full sequence is without end, but here are the first 12 terms:

1, 1, 2, 3, 5, 8, 13, 21, 34, 55, 89, 144...

Any given number in the sequence is approximately *0.618 x (the following number)* and *1.618 x (the preceding number)*. And it is these inter-relationships which followers of the Elliott Wave theory used to determine the wave count for predicting the period and magnitude and future stock market moves ranging from minutes though to decades. Exactly how to do this is obviously beyond the scope of this book, so instead I refer you to *The Elliott Wave Principle* by "Prechter and Frost" published in 1978.

Chapter 11

Chaos and the Future

In the early 1960's polish scientist Benoit Mandelbrot started work in the research wing of IBM Computers. Although he was essentially looking into electronic noise produced in the functioning of computers he was a mathematical jack-of-all-trades and had been dabbling in economics at the same time. He had gathered a fair amount of data and was preparing to give a lecture on the distribution of large and small incomes in the economy.

One day, when he was talking to a Harvard economics Professor about the lecture he was about to give he noticed a diagram on the Professor's blackboard. "How did you get hold of the diagram that I am going to use," asked Mandelbrot of the Professor. "I haven't," replied the Professor. Indeed the Professor knew nothing about Mandelbrot's research and had certainly not seen any of the diagrams from the forthcoming lecture. Instead the diagram that had been put on the blackboard represented eight years worth of cotton prices.

The similarity between the two diagrams perplexed Mandelbrot. Here were two, totally unrelated, sets of data showing a high degree of coincidence and similarity. How could it be that patterns in the distribution of incomes could be reflected in cotton prices? After all, the conventional thinking, which technical analysts will recognise, suggested that long term cotton prices would be driven by real forces in the economy such as the discovery of new trading partners and trade routes. And, in the short term, prices would move around in smaller cycles more dependent on conditions experienced in the growing seasons.

Mandelbrot took both sets of data and looked more closely at them. There were more large jumps in the price compared to small changes than would have been expected. A statistician, looking at this form of data, would have expected it to fit a bell-shaped curve known as Gaussian or normal distribution. These are the forms in which randomness is distributed according to classical science. Yet, no matter how Mandelbrot and the Professor plotted them, the cotton prices could not be made to fit either of these distributions. But as they plotted some of their charts Mandelbrot began to see the similarities with diagrams he had seen in other branches of his mathematical research - non-linear dynamic systems, or chaos.

The Department of Agriculture in Washington could provide cotton prices dating back to the 1900's. Complete records were available because the market was centralised and hence record keeping was also centralised. For virtually all of the century cotton had flowed through New York on route to New England, and Liverpool's prices were also linked to New York.

What Mandelbrot had discovered flew in the face of normal thinking. Everyone assumed that large, long term changes had nothing to do with the smaller, transient changes. The idea that rapid fluctuations were almost random, whereas long term fluctuations were determined by macro-economic forces, such as war and recession were almost cast in stone. Instead of separating the large and small scale changes, Mandelbrot's model firmly bound them together. He found patterns that repeated themselves, not just in one scale or another, but across every scale of the cotton price movements. Working at IBM he had access to some of the most powerful computing facilities at the time. Using them he was able to prove that the data which didn't fit into the normal distribution pattern produced symmetry from the point of view of scaling. In other words, although all of the price changes were supposedly random and unpredictable, the sequence of changes in the price of cotton were independent of scale. So the curves he produced for daily, monthly and annual price changes matched one another almost perfectly. That means that cotton price changes viewed on a Mandelbrot diagram had remained constant over a 60 year period despite the occurrence of two world wars and a massive recession.

Mandelbrot quickly moved onto other things, as was his way, but other mathematicians and economists took up where he left off. It has now been shown fairly conclusively that the capital markets are indeed non-linear, dynamic systems. They follow a chaotic nature and it should not be possible to forecast their next move. But within chaos there are patterns which can be shown on Mandelbrot diagrams

Trends do occur and it will always be possible to make money from them in the markets - it is not a requirement that you have to be able to predict the exact price at some point in the future. What-is-more the occurrence of patterns, such as reversal and consolidation patterns, is more than statistically significant. So, a technical approach to the market and careful money management will allow you to come out ahead of those who operate without a structured approach. In the same way that you know small items fall to the earth by the force of gravity but don't understand Newton's laws let alone Einstein's General Relativity, you can understand that patterns are repeating themselves on the stock market without understanding chaos theory and fractal geometry!

Chapter 12

Successful Chart Trading

There is a lot more to making money out of the financial markets than drawing charts and performing a couple of calculations. You also need to develop a state of mind that goes hand-in-hand with your approach to making money. Someone who believes in fundamentals and enjoys a cerebral approach to the markets will require a different strategy to someone who is willing to spend hours researching a company in search of value. And the technical analyst or chart trader will require a different mind set again. Here are a few of the characteristics of a successful chart trader. Perhaps they will prove useful in testing yourself to see if you really should be using technical analysis to help you in the markets, or you may wish to develop some of the characteristics to help you along your way.

Personal Risk Management

The first step in becoming a successful trader is deciding on what **level of risk** you feel happy with. Are you prepared to take high risks every time you make a trade or are you relatively risk averse and afraid of losing your money? If you are somewhere in between, decide now which way would you tend to lean if you had to choose one or the other.

This is truly a 'personal thing' and should not be influenced by any outside factors. There is nothing macho about being afraid of risk, so if you are truly worried by the prospect of losing all of your money then you need to admit it to yourself now.

Closely associated with risk management is the understanding of **why you want to trade in the first place.** Is it because you have simply got too much money and want a way of getting rid of it? Do you have a target of something that you wish to buy with the profits that you will make? Or do you simply want to achieve a better return on your money than by putting it into a building society?

This is all part of setting a benchmark so that you know how you are performing. You might make a few trades and a small profit and feel ecstatic about the fact. But you could be totally failing in your objectives and therefore need to change your approach. Likewise, you may take a few losses on your trades and feel as if the whole world is against you and it really is not worth the effort. But you could be exceeding your original expectations without really knowing it. In this situation, as well, you should really be changing your strategy for two reasons: You can afford to take a less risky approach to the markets because you are exceeding your aims, and that less risky approach will also let you sleep easier because you are obviously a worrier.

With your approach to risk and the reasons for trading firmly set in your mind, the next step is to decide what funds you are going to make available for trading. This should sensibly range between 1% and 10% of your total funds available for investment. The rest should be invested for the long term with no attempt being made to take advantage of peaks and troughs. Nearly all charts drawn in all markets for all times show that investing for long periods and ignoring set backs is a sensible strategy and will return better results than leaving your money on deposit.

Dealing with Uncertainty

The reason for choosing such a low percentage of your total investment funds is that there are no certainties in the financial markets. As a result the chart trader must learn to deal with uncertainty and the associated risks. Being wrong with a technical trading signal is all part of the business. Some days you will be "lucky" and some days you will be "unlucky". You never know just what's around the corner and when an "accident" is about to happen. All successful traders accept that one day they are going to get wiped out. Indeed, over their trading lifetime, they expect to get wiped out a number of times.

Remain Logical and Not Emotional

Because of the possibility of being wiped out you need to have certain plans in place. These plans don't just have to deal with when to buy a particular stock and how much to invest, but should also include a way of withdrawing profits from your trading account. There are two types of trader who are destined to always lose more than they make.

- ☹ The first will believe that they are on a winning streak and always plough all of their profits back into the market. They have no plan of withdrawing their profits and are always in the market at all times right up to the hilt. Every time they make a profit they give it back to the market until the market says, "enough is enough" and takes it all away.

- ☹ The second is the 'eternal optimist' who is always convinced that they know what is going to happen. When the market is dropping like a stone they insist on buying in preparation for the upturn. And when the market continues to fall instead of selling at their stop loss they buy even more because the new, lower market represents even more of a bargain. These people also sell into a runaway bull market because they can see a drop on the horizon. When the market keeps going they take an even shorter position because there is further for the market to fall.

Both of these traders lack a defined exit point with respect to their profits. One approach would be to remove 25% of your profits every year. Another could be to remove 50% of your profit every time you double your money. Whatever you decide, make a plan and stick to it.

The same should be said of the methods and techniques that you use for buying and selling your stocks.

Having read this book you now know the various signals that you will get from the market. Decide on the stocks that you would like to trade, the methods that you would like to use and those which you can fit in with your lifestyle. It is no good deciding that you are going to use Fibonacci sequences and Elliott Waves at the basis of your trading plan if you can only afford five minutes each day for studying prices. Also, if you don't have a computer, you will find the grind of calculating moving averages probably too much to bear.

Remain Focused

The charts that have been discussed serve as a guide or a 'road map' in the changing world of the markets. Over time you will become an expert at reading the particular signs that you decided to use. Perhaps in the early days they won't produce outstanding results, but as time goes by, you will become more accustomed to them and the exact way in which they work. You may even develop your own charting techniques as modifications to those contained in this book. Whatever they are you need to remain focused on what you are doing and not be swayed by extraneous information.

Patience, courage and persistence are essential characteristics for a successful trader. If you do get wiped out don't take it personally. Just shrug it off as one of those things that happen and get on with your next set of evaluations (not forgetting to figure out, logically, why it was that you did get wiped out). Do not give up. It takes years of trading experience to become successful. But when you do it will all become worthwhile.

Be Decisive

Putting all of these together you should now have a good degree of self knowledge and a cold approach to the market. You know that they are volatile and you know that you could get wiped out but you also know what you are going to do, how you are going to achieve it and how much you are going to make. There is now nothing in your way. Emotion does not come into it, so when you receive a signal to buy that is backed-up and has good authority you should buy. When a signal to sell is clear and authoritative you should sell.

A trading method can only succeed if it is followed **consistently and decisively**. Sometimes the trade will be good and other times not so good. But if you are indecisive and inconsistent you don't stand a chance of discovering what is going wrong and what is going right. And if you can't Figure out the right from the wrong you will not make progress and improve.

There is only one thing worse than getting it all wrong in the financial markets, and that is not knowing why you are getting it all wrong.

The Complete Beginner's Guide to The Internet

What exactly is The Internet? Where did it come from and where is it going? And, more importantly, how can everybody take their place in this new community?

The Complete Beginner's Guide to The Internet answers all of those questions and more. On top of being an indispensable guide to the basics of Cyberspace,

❑ It is the lowest priced introduction on the market by a long way at a surfer-friendly £4.95. Who wants to spend £30+ on an alternative to find out The Internet is not for them?

❑ It comes in an easy-to-read format. Alternatives, with their 300+ pages, are intimidating even to those who are familiar with The Net, let alone complete beginners!

Price: £4.95

- What types of resources are available for private, educational and business use,
- What software and hardware you need to access them,
- How to communicate with others, and
- The rules of the Superhighway, or 'netiquette'.

Find What You Want on the Internet

Locating information and other resources on the Internet can be very frustrating and time consuming. But it doesn't have to be that way. ***Find What You Want on The Internet*** is designed to teach Internet users — from novices to veterans — how to locate information quickly and easily.

❑ Which search techniques and Search Engines work best for your specific needs? ❑ What is the real difference between true 'search' sites and on-line directories, and how do you decide which one to use? ❑How do the world's most powerful Search Engines, such as Yahoo!, Alta Vista, Lycos, Infoseek and Excite, really work?

Price: £5-95

Understand
Shares
in a Day

Understand Shares in a Day is an indispensable title which shows how the share market really works. Inexperienced investors will learn:

❑ About different types of shares ... ❑ Why share prices fluctuate... ❑ How to read the financial pages ... ❑ How shares are bought and sold ... ❑ How risk can be spread with investment and unit trusts ... ❑ How to build a portfolio of shares ... ❑ The risks and rewards associated with Penny Shares

£6.95

Once this basic groundwork has been covered, the book explores more complex ideas which will appeal to both beginners and more experienced investors alike, including: ● How to value shares ● How equity options are used by professional investors to 'gear' profits and hedge against falling share prices.

£6.95

Understand
Commodities
in a Day

An easy-to-read introduction to the subject. With plenty of simple examples it lifts the mysteries of trading in grains, livestock, precious and industrial metals, petroleum, lumber, coffee, sugar, soyabeans, etc., etc.

This handy title shows potential new traders, and those with an interest in the commodities markets, how to assess and calculate the risks and rewards, giving simple-to-follow sets of criteria on which to base buying and selling decisions.

Learn... ❑ The basic concept of commodity trading... ❑ How to calculate profits and losses... ❑ Physical commodity contract specifications... ❑ How to place a properly executable order in the market... ❑ Four trading strategies from the experts

Understand
Derivatives
in a Day

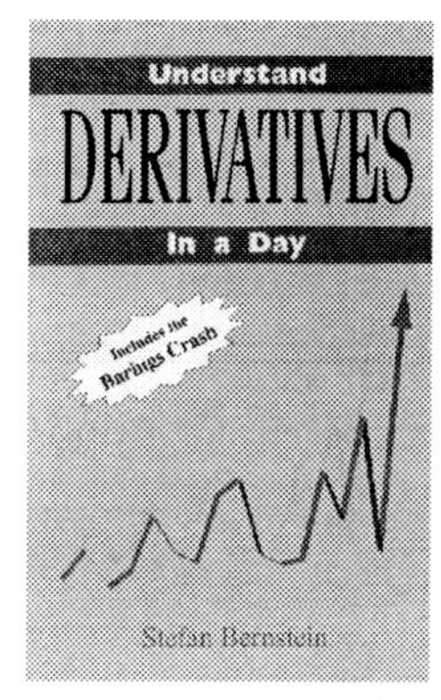

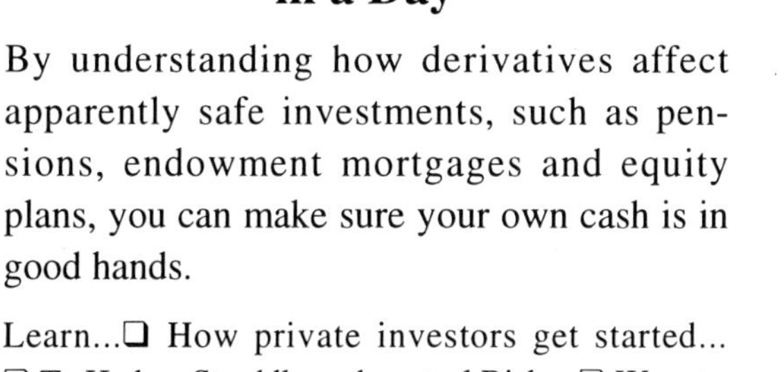

By understanding how derivatives affect apparently safe investments, such as pensions, endowment mortgages and equity plans, you can make sure your own cash is in good hands.

£6.95

Learn...❑ How private investors get started... ❑ To Hedge, Straddle and control Risk... ❑ Ways to limit the downside but *not* the upside... ❑ About *risk free* derivative strategies... ❑ Trading Psychology - Fear, Hope and Greed... ❑ Also, the History of Derivatives; Currency Speculation; Long and Short puts; Tarantula Trading; and much more.

Understand
Bonds and Gilts
in a Day

This handy title shows potential investors, and those with an interest in the bond markets, how to assess the potential risks and rewards, giving a simple to follow set of criteria on which to base investment decisions. The confusing terminology used in the bond market is clearly explained with working definitions of many terms and a comprehensive glossary.

£6.95

For the more seasoned bond and gilt investor there are sets of bond strategies laid out so the reader can evaluate their holdings and pick a course of investment which best suits their needs.

Using illustrations and examples *Understand Bonds and Gilts in a Day* shows how investors can ❑guard against default by the issuer, ❑diversify a portfolio to smooth delayed payments of interest ❑determine which bonds and gilts are carrying a premium and which a discount ❑avoid the liquidity risk of rising interest rates